ISBN 0-8373-3149-8

C-3149   CAREER EXAMINATION SERIES

This is your
PASSBOOK® for...

Evidence Control Clerk

Test Preparation Study Guide

Questions & Answers

NATIONAL LEARNING CORPORATION

PASSBOOK®
NOTICE

PASSBOOK® SERIES

THE *PASSBOOK® SERIES* has been created to prepare applicants and candidates for the ultimate academic battlefield – the examination room.

At some time in our lives, each and every one of us may be required to take an examination – for validation, matriculation, admission, qualification, registration, certification, or licensure.

Based on the assumption that every applicant or candidate has met the basic formal educational standards, has taken the required number of courses, and read the necessary texts, the *PASSBOOK® SERIES* furnishes the one special preparation which may assure passing with confidence, instead of failing with insecurity. Examination questions – together with answers – are furnished as the basic vehicle for study so that the mysteries of the examination and its compounding difficulties may be eliminated or diminished by a sure method.

This book is meant to help you pass your examination provided that you qualify and are serious in your objective.

The entire field is reviewed through the huge store of content information which is succinctly presented through a provocative and challenging approach – the question-and-answer method.

A climate of success is established by furnishing the correct answers at the end of each test.

You soon learn to recognize types of questions, forms of questions, and patterns of questioning. You may even begin to anticipate expected outcomes.

You perceive that many questions are repeated or adapted so that you can gain acute insights, which may enable you to score many sure points.

You learn how to confront new questions, or types of questions, and to attack them confidently and work out the correct answers.

You note objectives and emphases, and recognize pitfalls and dangers, so that you may make positive educational adjustments.

Moreover, you are kept fully informed in relation to new concepts, methods, practices, and directions in the field.

You discover that you are actually taking the examination all the time: you are preparing for the examination by "taking" an examination, not by reading extraneous and/or supererogatory textbooks.

In short, this PASSBOOK®, used directedly, should be an important factor in helping you to pass your test.

EVIDENCE CONTROL CLERK

DUTIES

Under supervision, perform responsible work involving security, courier and storage functions for the transport, inspection, storage and delivery of legal and illegal substances and property such as firearms, narcotics, cash, jewelry, etc., being held in evidence by the Police Department or the Medical Examiner; and perform related work.

TEST

The multiple-choice test may include questions on reading comprehension; deductive reasoning; information ordering/prioritization; clerical skills, including file management and proofreading; basic arithmetic; and other related areas.

HOW TO TAKE A TEST

I. YOU MUST PASS AN EXAMINATION

A. WHAT EVERY CANDIDATE SHOULD KNOW

Examination applicants often ask us for help in preparing for the written test. What can I study in advance? What kinds of questions will be asked? How will the test be given? How will the papers be graded?

As an applicant for a civil service examination, you may be wondering about some of these things. Our purpose here is to suggest effective methods of advance study and to describe civil service examinations.

Your chances for success on this examination can be increased if you know how to prepare. Those "pre-examination jitters" can be reduced if you know what to expect. You can even experience an adventure in good citizenship if you know why civil service exams are given.

B. WHY ARE CIVIL SERVICE EXAMINATIONS GIVEN?

Civil service examinations are important to you in two ways. As a citizen, you want public jobs filled by employees who know how to do their work. As a job seeker, you want a fair chance to compete for that job on an equal footing with other candidates. The best-known means of accomplishing this two-fold goal is the competitive examination.

Exams are widely publicized throughout the nation. They may be administered for jobs in federal, state, city, municipal, town or village governments or agencies.

Any citizen may apply, with some limitations, such as the age or residence of applicants. Your experience and education may be reviewed to see whether you meet the requirements for the particular examination. When these requirements exist, they are reasonable and applied consistently to all applicants. Thus, a competitive examination may cause you some uneasiness now, but it is your privilege and safeguard.

C. HOW ARE CIVIL SERVICE EXAMS DEVELOPED?

Examinations are carefully written by trained technicians who are specialists in the field known as "psychological measurement," in consultation with recognized authorities in the field of work that the test will cover. These experts recommend the subject matter areas or skills to be tested; only those knowledges or skills important to your success on the job are included. The most reliable books and source materials available are used as references. Together, the experts and technicians judge the difficulty level of the questions.

Test technicians know how to phrase questions so that the problem is clearly stated. Their ethics do not permit "trick" or "catch" questions. Questions may have been tried out on sample groups, or subjected to statistical analysis, to determine their usefulness.

Written tests are often used in combination with performance tests, ratings of training and experience, and oral interviews. All of these measures combine to form the best-known means of finding the right person for the right job.

II. HOW TO PASS THE WRITTEN TEST

A. NATURE OF THE EXAMINATION

To prepare intelligently for civil service examinations, you should know how they differ from school examinations you have taken. In school you were assigned certain definite pages to read or subjects to cover. The examination questions were quite detailed and usually emphasized memory. Civil service exams, on the other hand, try to discover your present ability to perform the duties of a position, plus your potentiality to learn these duties. In other words, a civil service exam attempts to predict how successful you will be. Questions cover such a broad area that they cannot be as minute and detailed as school exam questions.

In the public service similar kinds of work, or positions, are grouped together in one "class." This process is known as *position-classification*. All the positions in a class are paid according to the salary range for that class. One class title covers all of these positions, and they are all tested by the same examination.

B. FOUR BASIC STEPS

1) Study the announcement

How, then, can you know what subjects to study? Our best answer is: "Learn as much as possible about the class of positions for which you've applied." The exam will test the knowledge, skills and abilities needed to do the work.

Your most valuable source of information about the position you want is the official exam announcement. This announcement lists the training and experience qualifications. Check these standards and apply only if you come reasonably close to meeting them.

The brief description of the position in the examination announcement offers some clues to the subjects which will be tested. Think about the job itself. Review the duties in your mind. Can you perform them, or are there some in which you are rusty? Fill in the blank spots in your preparation.

Many jurisdictions preview the written test in the exam announcement by including a section called "Knowledge and Abilities Required," "Scope of the Examination," or some similar heading. Here you will find out specifically what fields will be tested.

2) Review your own background

Once you learn in general what the position is all about, and what you need to know to do the work, ask yourself which subjects you already know fairly well and which need improvement. You may wonder whether to concentrate on improving your strong areas or on building some background in your fields of weakness. When the announcement has specified "some knowledge" or "considerable knowledge," or has used adjectives like "beginning principles of…" or "advanced … methods," you can get a clue as to the number and difficulty of questions to be asked in any given field. More questions, and hence broader coverage, would be included for those subjects which are more important in the work. Now weigh your strengths and weaknesses against the job requirements and prepare accordingly.

3) Determine the level of the position

Another way to tell how intensively you should prepare is to understand the level of the job for which you are applying. Is it the entering level? In other words, is this the position in which beginners in a field of work are hired? Or is it an intermediate or advanced level? Sometimes this is indicated by such words as "Junior" or "Senior" in the class title. Other jurisdictions use Roman numerals to designate the level – Clerk I, Clerk II, for example. The word "Supervisor" sometimes appears in the title. If the level is not indicated by the title, check the description of duties. Will you be working under very close supervision, or will you have responsibility for independent decisions in this work?

4) Choose appropriate study materials

Now that you know the subjects to be examined and the relative amount of each subject to be covered, you can choose suitable study materials. For beginning level jobs, or even advanced ones, if you have a pronounced weakness in some aspect of your training, read a modern, standard textbook in that field. Be sure it is up to date and has general coverage. Such books are normally available at your library, and the librarian will be glad to help you locate one. For entry-level positions, questions of appropriate difficulty are chosen – neither highly advanced questions, nor those too simple. Such questions require careful thought but not advanced training.

If the position for which you are applying is technical or advanced, you will read more advanced, specialized material. If you are already familiar with the basic principles of your field, elementary textbooks would waste your time. Concentrate on advanced textbooks and technical periodicals. Think through the concepts and review difficult problems in your field.

These are all general sources. You can get more ideas on your own initiative, following these leads. For example, training manuals and publications of the government agency which employs workers in your field can be useful, particularly for technical and professional positions. A letter or visit to the government department involved may result in more specific study suggestions, and certainly will provide you with a more definite idea of the exact nature of the position you are seeking.

III. KINDS OF TESTS

Tests are used for purposes other than measuring knowledge and ability to perform specified duties. For some positions, it is equally important to test ability to make adjustments to new situations or to profit from training. In others, basic mental abilities not dependent on information are essential. Questions which test these things may not appear as pertinent to the duties of the position as those which test for knowledge and information. Yet they are often highly important parts of a fair examination. For very general questions, it is almost impossible to help you direct your study efforts. What we can do is to point out some of the more common of these general abilities needed in public service positions and describe some typical questions.

1) General information

Broad, general information has been found useful for predicting job success in some kinds of work. This is tested in a variety of ways, from vocabulary lists to questions about current events. Basic background in some field of work, such as sociology or economics, may be sampled in a group of questions. Often these are principles which have become familiar to most persons through exposure rather than through formal training. It is difficult to advise you how to study for these questions; being alert to the world around you is our best suggestion.

2) Verbal ability

An example of an ability needed in many positions is verbal or language ability. Verbal ability is, in brief, the ability to use and understand words. Vocabulary and grammar tests are typical measures of this ability. Reading comprehension or paragraph interpretation questions are common in many kinds of civil service tests. You are given a paragraph of written material and asked to find its central meaning.

3) Numerical ability

Number skills can be tested by the familiar arithmetic problem, by checking paired lists of numbers to see which are alike and which are different, or by interpreting charts and graphs. In the latter test, a graph may be printed in the test booklet which you are asked to use as the basis for answering questions.

4) Observation

A popular test for law-enforcement positions is the observation test. A picture is shown to you for several minutes, then taken away. Questions about the picture test your ability to observe both details and larger elements.

5) Following directions

In many positions in the public service, the employee must be able to carry out written instructions dependably and accurately. You may be given a chart with several columns, each column listing a variety of information. The questions require you to carry out directions involving the information given in the chart.

6) Skills and aptitudes

Performance tests effectively measure some manual skills and aptitudes. When the skill is one in which you are trained, such as typing or shorthand, you can practice. These tests are often very much like those given in business school or high school courses. For many of the other skills and aptitudes, however, no short-time preparation can be made. Skills and abilities natural to you or that you have developed throughout your lifetime are being tested.

Many of the general questions just described provide all the data needed to answer the questions and ask you to use your reasoning ability to find the answers. Your best preparation for these tests, as well as for tests of facts and ideas, is to be at your physical and mental best. You, no doubt, have your own methods of getting into an exam-taking mood and keeping "in shape." The next section lists some ideas on this subject.

IV. KINDS OF QUESTIONS

Only rarely is the "essay" question, which you answer in narrative form, used in civil service tests. Civil service tests are usually of the short-answer type. Full instructions for answering these questions will be given to you at the examination. But in case this is your first experience with short-answer questions and separate answer sheets, here is what you need to know:

1) Multiple-choice Questions

Most popular of the short-answer questions is the "multiple choice" or "best answer" question. It can be used, for example, to test for factual knowledge, ability to solve problems or judgment in meeting situations found at work.

A multiple-choice question is normally one of three types—

- It can begin with an incomplete statement followed by several possible endings. You are to find the one ending which *best* completes the statement, although some of the others may not be entirely wrong.
- It can also be a complete statement in the form of a question which is answered by choosing one of the statements listed.

- It can be in the form of a problem – again you select the best answer.

Here is an example of a multiple-choice question with a discussion which should give you some clues as to the method for choosing the right answer:

When an employee has a complaint about his assignment, the action which will *best* help him overcome his difficulty is to
  - A. discuss his difficulty with his coworkers
  - B. take the problem to the head of the organization
  - C. take the problem to the person who gave him the assignment
  - D. say nothing to anyone about his complaint

In answering this question, you should study each of the choices to find which is best. Consider choice "A" – Certainly an employee may discuss his complaint with fellow employees, but no change or improvement can result, and the complaint remains unresolved. Choice "B" is a poor choice since the head of the organization probably does not know what assignment you have been given, and taking your problem to him is known as "going over the head" of the supervisor. The supervisor, or person who made the assignment, is the person who can clarify it or correct any injustice. Choice "C" is, therefore, correct. To say nothing, as in choice "D," is unwise. Supervisors have and interest in knowing the problems employees are facing, and the employee is seeking a solution to his problem.

2) True/False Questions

The "true/false" or "right/wrong" form of question is sometimes used. Here a complete statement is given. Your job is to decide whether the statement is right or wrong.

SAMPLE: A roaming cell-phone call to a nearby city costs less than a non-roaming call to a distant city.

This statement is wrong, or false, since roaming calls are more expensive.

This is not a complete list of all possible question forms, although most of the others are variations of these common types. You will always get complete directions for answering questions. Be sure you understand *how* to mark your answers – ask questions until you do.

V. RECORDING YOUR ANSWERS

Computer terminals are used more and more today for many different kinds of exams.

For an examination with very few applicants, you may be told to record your answers in the test booklet itself. Separate answer sheets are much more common. If this separate answer sheet is to be scored by machine – and this is often the case – it is highly important that you mark your answers correctly in order to get credit.

An electronic scoring machine is often used in civil service offices because of the speed with which papers can be scored. Machine-scored answer sheets must be marked with a pencil, which will be given to you. This pencil has a high graphite content which responds to the electronic scoring machine. As a matter of fact, stray dots may register as answers, so do not let your pencil rest on the answer sheet while you are pondering the correct answer. Also, if your pencil lead breaks or is otherwise defective, ask for another.

Since the answer sheet will be dropped in a slot in the scoring machine, be careful not to bend the corners or get the paper crumpled.

The answer sheet normally has five vertical columns of numbers, with 30 numbers to a column. These numbers correspond to the question numbers in your test booklet. After each number, going across the page are four or five pairs of dotted lines. These short dotted lines have small letters or numbers above them. The first two pairs may also have a "T" or "F" above the letters. This indicates that the first two pairs only are to be used if the questions are of the true-false type. If the questions are multiple choice, disregard the "T" and "F" and pay attention only to the small letters or numbers.

Answer your questions in the manner of the sample that follows:

32. The largest city in the United States is
    A. Washington, D.C.
    B. New York City
    C. Chicago
    D. Detroit
    E. San Francisco

1) Choose the answer you think is best. (New York City is the largest, so "B" is correct.)
2) Find the row of dotted lines numbered the same as the question you are answering. (Find row number 32)
3) Find the pair of dotted lines corresponding to the answer. (Find the pair of lines under the mark "B.")
4) Make a solid black mark between the dotted lines.

VI. BEFORE THE TEST

Common sense will help you find procedures to follow to get ready for an examination. Too many of us, however, overlook these sensible measures. Indeed, nervousness and fatigue have been found to be the most serious reasons why applicants fail to do their best on civil service tests. Here is a list of reminders:

- Begin your preparation early – Don't wait until the last minute to go scurrying around for books and materials or to find out what the position is all about.
- Prepare continuously – An hour a night for a week is better than an all-night cram session. This has been definitely established. What is more, a night a week for a month will return better dividends than crowding your study into a shorter period of time.
- Locate the place of the exam – You have been sent a notice telling you when and where to report for the examination. If the location is in a different town or otherwise unfamiliar to you, it would be well to inquire the best route and learn something about the building.
- Relax the night before the test – Allow your mind to rest. Do not study at all that night. Plan some mild recreation or diversion; then go to bed early and get a good night's sleep.
- Get up early enough to make a leisurely trip to the place for the test – This way unforeseen events, traffic snarls, unfamiliar buildings, etc. will not upset you.
- Dress comfortably – A written test is not a fashion show. You will be known by number and not by name, so wear something comfortable.

- Leave excess paraphernalia at home – Shopping bags and odd bundles will get in your way. You need bring only the items mentioned in the official notice you received; usually everything you need is provided. Do not bring reference books to the exam. They will only confuse those last minutes and be taken away from you when in the test room.
- Arrive somewhat ahead of time – If because of transportation schedules you must get there very early, bring a newspaper or magazine to take your mind off yourself while waiting.
- Locate the examination room – When you have found the proper room, you will be directed to the seat or part of the room where you will sit. Sometimes you are given a sheet of instructions to read while you are waiting. Do not fill out any forms until you are told to do so; just read them and be prepared.
- Relax and prepare to listen to the instructions
- If you have any physical problem that may keep you from doing your best, be sure to tell the test administrator. If you are sick or in poor health, you really cannot do your best on the exam. You can come back and take the test some other time.

VII. AT THE TEST

The day of the test is here and you have the test booklet in your hand. The temptation to get going is very strong. Caution! There is more to success than knowing the right answers. You must know how to identify your papers and understand variations in the type of short-answer question used in this particular examination. Follow these suggestions for maximum results from your efforts:

1) Cooperate with the monitor
The test administrator has a duty to create a situation in which you can be as much at ease as possible. He will give instructions, tell you when to begin, check to see that you are marking your answer sheet correctly, and so on. He is not there to guard you, although he will see that your competitors do not take unfair advantage. He wants to help you do your best.

2) Listen to all instructions
Don't jump the gun! Wait until you understand all directions. In most civil service tests you get more time than you need to answer the questions. So don't be in a hurry. Read each word of instructions until you clearly understand the meaning. Study the examples, listen to all announcements and follow directions. Ask questions if you do not understand what to do.

3) Identify your papers
Civil service exams are usually identified by number only. You will be assigned a number; you must not put your name on your test papers. Be sure to copy your number correctly. Since more than one exam may be given, copy your exact examination title.

4) Plan your time
Unless you are told that a test is a "speed" or "rate of work" test, speed itself is usually not important. Time enough to answer all the questions will be provided, but this does not mean that you have all day. An overall time limit has been set. Divide the total time (in minutes) by the number of questions to determine the approximate time you have for each question.

5) Do not linger over difficult questions

If you come across a difficult question, mark it with a paper clip (useful to have along) and come back to it when you have been through the booklet. One caution if you do this – be sure to skip a number on your answer sheet as well. Check often to be sure that you have not lost your place and that you are marking in the row numbered the same as the question you are answering.

6) Read the questions

Be sure you know what the question asks! Many capable people are unsuccessful because they failed to *read* the questions correctly.

7) Answer all questions

Unless you have been instructed that a penalty will be deducted for incorrect answers, it is better to guess than to omit a question.

8) Speed tests

It is often better NOT to guess on speed tests. It has been found that on timed tests people are tempted to spend the last few seconds before time is called in marking answers at random – without even reading them – in the hope of picking up a few extra points. To discourage this practice, the instructions may warn you that your score will be "corrected" for guessing. That is, a penalty will be applied. The incorrect answers will be deducted from the correct ones, or some other penalty formula will be used.

9) Review your answers

If you finish before time is called, go back to the questions you guessed or omitted to give them further thought. Review other answers if you have time.

10) Return your test materials

If you are ready to leave before others have finished or time is called, take ALL your materials to the monitor and leave quietly. Never take any test material with you. The monitor can discover whose papers are not complete, and taking a test booklet may be grounds for disqualification.

VIII. EXAMINATION TECHNIQUES

1) Read the general instructions carefully. These are usually printed on the first page of the exam booklet. As a rule, these instructions refer to the timing of the examination; the fact that you should not start work until the signal and must stop work at a signal, etc. If there are any *special* instructions, such as a choice of questions to be answered, make sure that you note this instruction carefully.

2) When you are ready to start work on the examination, that is as soon as the signal has been given, read the instructions to each question booklet, underline any key words or phrases, such as *least, best, outline, describe* and the like. In this way you will tend to answer as requested rather than discover on reviewing your paper that you *listed without describing*, that you selected the *worst* choice rather than the *best* choice, etc.

3) If the examination is of the objective or multiple-choice type – that is, each question will also give a series of possible answers: A, B, C or D, and you are called upon to select the best answer and write the letter next to that answer on your answer paper – it is advisable to start answering each question in turn. There may be anywhere from 50 to 100 such questions in the three or four hours allotted and you can see how much time would be taken if you read through all the questions before beginning to answer any. Furthermore, if you come across a question or group of questions which you know would be difficult to answer, it would undoubtedly affect your handling of all the other questions.

4) If the examination is of the essay type and contains but a few questions, it is a moot point as to whether you should read all the questions before starting to answer any one. Of course, if you are given a choice – say five out of seven and the like – then it is essential to read all the questions so you can eliminate the two that are most difficult. If, however, you are asked to answer all the questions, there may be danger in trying to answer the easiest one first because you may find that you will spend too much time on it. The best technique is to answer the first question, then proceed to the second, etc.

5) Time your answers. Before the exam begins, write down the time it started, then add the time allowed for the examination and write down the time it must be completed, then divide the time available somewhat as follows:
   - If 3-1/2 hours are allowed, that would be 210 minutes. If you have 80 objective-type questions, that would be an average of 2-1/2 minutes per question. Allow yourself no more than 2 minutes per question, or a total of 160 minutes, which will permit about 50 minutes to review.
   - If for the time allotment of 210 minutes there are 7 essay questions to answer, that would average about 30 minutes a question. Give yourself only 25 minutes per question so that you have about 35 minutes to review.

6) The most important instruction is to *read each question* and make sure you know what is wanted. The second most important instruction is to *time yourself properly* so that you answer every question. The third most important instruction is to *answer every question*. Guess if you have to but include something for each question. Remember that you will receive no credit for a blank and will probably receive some credit if you write something in answer to an essay question. If you guess a letter – say "B" for a multiple-choice question – you may have guessed right. If you leave a blank as an answer to a multiple-choice question, the examiners may respect your feelings but it will not add a point to your score. Some exams may penalize you for wrong answers, so in such cases *only*, you may not want to guess unless you have some basis for your answer.

7) Suggestions
   a. Objective-type questions
      1. Examine the question booklet for proper sequence of pages and questions
      2. Read all instructions carefully
      3. Skip any question which seems too difficult; return to it after all other questions have been answered
      4. Apportion your time properly; do not spend too much time on any single question or group of questions

5. Note and underline key words – *all, most, fewest, least, best, worst, same, opposite,* etc.
6. Pay particular attention to negatives
7. Note unusual option, e.g., unduly long, short, complex, different or similar in content to the body of the question
8. Observe the use of "hedging" words – *probably, may, most likely,* etc.
9. Make sure that your answer is put next to the same number as the question
10. Do not second-guess unless you have good reason to believe the second answer is definitely more correct
11. Cross out original answer if you decide another answer is more accurate; do not erase until you are ready to hand your paper in
12. Answer all questions; guess unless instructed otherwise
13. Leave time for review

   b. Essay questions
1. Read each question carefully
2. Determine exactly what is wanted. Underline key words or phrases.
3. Decide on outline or paragraph answer
4. Include many different points and elements unless asked to develop any one or two points or elements
5. Show impartiality by giving pros and cons unless directed to select one side only
6. Make and write down any assumptions you find necessary to answer the questions
7. Watch your English, grammar, punctuation and choice of words
8. Time your answers; don't crowd material

8) Answering the essay question

Most essay questions can be answered by framing the specific response around several key words or ideas. Here are a few such key words or ideas:

M's: manpower, materials, methods, money, management
P's: purpose, program, policy, plan, procedure, practice, problems, pitfalls, personnel, public relations
   a. Six basic steps in handling problems:
1. Preliminary plan and background development
2. Collect information, data and facts
3. Analyze and interpret information, data and facts
4. Analyze and develop solutions as well as make recommendations
5. Prepare report and sell recommendations
6. Install recommendations and follow up effectiveness

   b. Pitfalls to avoid
1. *Taking things for granted* – A statement of the situation does not necessarily imply that each of the elements is necessarily true; for example, a complaint may be invalid and biased so that all that can be taken for granted is that a complaint has been registered

2. *Considering only one side of a situation* – Wherever possible, indicate several alternatives and then point out the reasons you selected the best one
3. *Failing to indicate follow up* – Whenever your answer indicates action on your part, make certain that you will take proper follow-up action to see how successful your recommendations, procedures or actions turn out to be
4. *Taking too long in answering any single question* – Remember to time your answers properly

IX. AFTER THE TEST

Scoring procedures differ in detail among civil service jurisdictions although the general principles are the same. Whether the papers are hand-scored or graded by machine we have described, they are nearly always graded by number. That is, the person who marks the paper knows only the number – never the name – of the applicant. Not until all the papers have been graded will they be matched with names. If other tests, such as training and experience or oral interview ratings have been given, scores will be combined. Different parts of the examination usually have different weights. For example, the written test might count 60 percent of the final grade, and a rating of training and experience 40 percent. In many jurisdictions, veterans will have a certain number of points added to their grades.

After the final grade has been determined, the names are placed in grade order and an eligible list is established. There are various methods for resolving ties between those who get the same final grade – probably the most common is to place first the name of the person whose application was received first. Job offers are made from the eligible list in the order the names appear on it. You will be notified of your grade and your rank as soon as all these computations have been made. This will be done as rapidly as possible.

People who are found to meet the requirements in the announcement are called "eligibles." Their names are put on a list of eligible candidates. An eligible's chances of getting a job depend on how high he stands on this list and how fast agencies are filling jobs from the list.

When a job is to be filled from a list of eligibles, the agency asks for the names of people on the list of eligibles for that job. When the civil service commission receives this request, it sends to the agency the names of the three people highest on this list. Or, if the job to be filled has specialized requirements, the office sends the agency the names of the top three persons who meet these requirements from the general list.

The appointing officer makes a choice from among the three people whose names were sent to him. If the selected person accepts the appointment, the names of the others are put back on the list to be considered for future openings.

That is the rule in hiring from all kinds of eligible lists, whether they are for typist, carpenter, chemist, or something else. For every vacancy, the appointing officer has his choice of any one of the top three eligibles on the list. This explains why the person whose name is on top of the list sometimes does not get an appointment when some of the persons lower on the list do. If the appointing officer chooses the second or third eligible, the No. 1 eligible does not get a job at once, but stays on the list until he is appointed or the list is terminated.

X. HOW TO PASS THE INTERVIEW TEST

The examination for which you applied requires an oral interview test. You have already taken the written test and you are now being called for the interview test – the final part of the formal examination.

You may think that it is not possible to prepare for an interview test and that there are no procedures to follow during an interview. Our purpose is to point out some things you can do in advance that will help you and some good rules to follow and pitfalls to avoid while you are being interviewed.

What is an interview supposed to test?

The written examination is designed to test the technical knowledge and competence of the candidate; the oral is designed to evaluate intangible qualities, not readily measured otherwise, and to establish a list showing the relative fitness of each candidate – as measured against his competitors – for the position sought. Scoring is not on the basis of "right" and "wrong," but on a sliding scale of values ranging from "not passable" to "outstanding." As a matter of fact, it is possible to achieve a relatively low score without a single "incorrect" answer because of evident weakness in the qualities being measured.

Occasionally, an examination may consist entirely of an oral test – either an individual or a group oral. In such cases, information is sought concerning the technical knowledges and abilities of the candidate, since there has been no written examination for this purpose. More commonly, however, an oral test is used to supplement a written examination.

Who conducts interviews?

The composition of oral boards varies among different jurisdictions. In nearly all, a representative of the personnel department serves as chairman. One of the members of the board may be a representative of the department in which the candidate would work. In some cases, "outside experts" are used, and, frequently, a businessman or some other representative of the general public is asked to serve. Labor and management or other special groups may be represented. The aim is to secure the services of experts in the appropriate field.

However the board is composed, it is a good idea (and not at all improper or unethical) to ascertain in advance of the interview who the members are and what groups they represent. When you are introduced to them, you will have some idea of their backgrounds and interests, and at least you will not stutter and stammer over their names.

What should be done before the interview?

While knowledge about the board members is useful and takes some of the surprise element out of the interview, there is other preparation which is more substantive. It *is* possible to prepare for an oral interview – in several ways:

1) Keep a copy of your application and review it carefully before the interview

This may be the only document before the oral board, and the starting point of the interview. Know what education and experience you have listed there, and the sequence and dates of all of it. Sometimes the board will ask you to review the highlights of your experience for them; you should not have to hem and haw doing it.

2) Study the class specification and the examination announcement

Usually, the oral board has one or both of these to guide them. The qualities, characteristics or knowledges required by the position sought are stated in these documents. They offer valuable clues as to the nature of the oral interview. For example, if the job involves supervisory responsibilities, the announcement will usually indicate that knowledge of modern supervisory methods and the qualifications of the candidate as a supervisor will be tested. If so, you can expect such questions, frequently in the form of a hypothetical situation which you are expected to solve. NEVER go into an oral without knowledge of the duties and responsibilities of the job you seek.

3) Think through each qualification required

Try to visualize the kind of questions you would ask if you were a board member. How well could you answer them? Try especially to appraise your own knowledge and background in each area, *measured against the job sought*, and identify any areas in which you are weak. Be critical and realistic – do not flatter yourself.

4) Do some general reading in areas in which you feel you may be weak

For example, if the job involves supervision and your past experience has NOT, some general reading in supervisory methods and practices, particularly in the field of human relations, might be useful. Do NOT study agency procedures or detailed manuals. The oral board will be testing your understanding and capacity, not your memory.

5) Get a good night's sleep and watch your general health and mental attitude

You will want a clear head at the interview. Take care of a cold or any other minor ailment, and of course, no hangovers.

What should be done on the day of the interview?

Now comes the day of the interview itself. Give yourself plenty of time to get there. Plan to arrive somewhat ahead of the scheduled time, particularly if your appointment is in the fore part of the day. If a previous candidate fails to appear, the board might be ready for you a bit early. By early afternoon an oral board is almost invariably behind schedule if there are many candidates, and you may have to wait. Take along a book or magazine to read, or your application to review, but leave any extraneous material in the waiting room when you go in for your interview. In any event, relax and compose yourself.

The matter of dress is important. The board is forming impressions about you – from your experience, your manners, your attitude, and your appearance. Give your personal appearance careful attention. Dress your best, but not your flashiest. Choose conservative, appropriate clothing, and be sure it is immaculate. This is a business interview, and your appearance should indicate that you regard it as such. Besides, being well groomed and properly dressed will help boost your confidence.

Sooner or later, someone will call your name and escort you into the interview room. *This is it.* From here on you are on your own. It is too late for any more preparation. But remember, you asked for this opportunity to prove your fitness, and you are here because your request was granted.

What happens when you go in?

The usual sequence of events will be as follows: The clerk (who is often the board stenographer) will introduce you to the chairman of the oral board, who will introduce you to the other members of the board. Acknowledge the introductions before you sit down. Do not be surprised if you find a microphone facing you or a stenotypist sitting by. Oral interviews are usually recorded in the event of an appeal or other review.

Usually the chairman of the board will open the interview by reviewing the highlights of your education and work experience from your application – primarily for the benefit of the other members of the board, as well as to get the material into the record. Do not interrupt or comment unless there is an error or significant misinterpretation; if that is the case, do not hesitate. But do not quibble about insignificant matters. Also, he will usually ask you some question about your education, experience or your present job – partly to get you to start talking and to establish the interviewing "rapport." He may start the actual questioning, or turn it over to one of the other members. Frequently, each member undertakes the questioning on a particular area, one in which he is perhaps most competent, so you can expect each member to participate in the examination. Because time is limited, you may also expect some rather abrupt switches in the direction the questioning takes, so do not be upset by it. Normally, a board member will not pursue a single line of questioning unless he discovers a particular strength or weakness.

After each member has participated, the chairman will usually ask whether any member has any further questions, then will ask you if you have anything you wish to add. Unless you are expecting this question, it may floor you. Worse, it may start you off on an extended, extemporaneous speech. The board is not usually seeking more information. The question is principally to offer you a last opportunity to present further qualifications or to indicate that you have nothing to add. So, if you feel that a significant qualification or characteristic has been overlooked, it is proper to point it out in a sentence or so. Do not compliment the board on the thoroughness of their examination – they have been sketchy, and you know it. If you wish, merely say, "No thank you, I have nothing further to add." This is a point where you can "talk yourself out" of a good impression or fail to present an important bit of information. Remember, *you close the interview yourself.*

The chairman will then say, "That is all, Mr. _____, thank you." Do not be startled; the interview is over, and quicker than you think. Thank him, gather your belongings and take your leave. Save your sigh of relief for the other side of the door.

How to put your best foot forward

Throughout this entire process, you may feel that the board individually and collectively is trying to pierce your defenses, seek out your hidden weaknesses and embarrass and confuse you. Actually, this is not true. They are obliged to make an appraisal of your qualifications for the job you are seeking, and they want to see you in your best light. Remember, they must interview all candidates and a non-cooperative candidate may become a failure in spite of their best efforts to bring out his qualifications. Here are 15 suggestions that will help you:

1) Be natural – Keep your attitude confident, not cocky

If you are not confident that you can do the job, do not expect the board to be. Do not apologize for your weaknesses, try to bring out your strong points. The board is interested in a positive, not negative, presentation. Cockiness will antagonize any board member and make him wonder if you are covering up a weakness by a false show of strength.

2) Get comfortable, but don't lounge or sprawl

Sit erectly but not stiffly. A careless posture may lead the board to conclude that you are careless in other things, or at least that you are not impressed by the importance of the occasion. Either conclusion is natural, even if incorrect. Do not fuss with your clothing, a pencil or an ashtray. Your hands may occasionally be useful to emphasize a point; do not let them become a point of distraction.

3) Do not wisecrack or make small talk

This is a serious situation, and your attitude should show that you consider it as such. Further, the time of the board is limited – they do not want to waste it, and neither should you.

4) Do not exaggerate your experience or abilities

In the first place, from information in the application or other interviews and sources, the board may know more about you than you think. Secondly, you probably will not get away with it. An experienced board is rather adept at spotting such a situation, so do not take the chance.

5) If you know a board member, do not make a point of it, yet do not hide it

Certainly you are not fooling him, and probably not the other members of the board. Do not try to take advantage of your acquaintanceship – it will probably do you little good.

6) Do not dominate the interview

Let the board do that. They will give you the clues – do not assume that you have to do all the talking. Realize that the board has a number of questions to ask you, and do not try to take up all the interview time by showing off your extensive knowledge of the answer to the first one.

7) Be attentive

You only have 20 minutes or so, and you should keep your attention at its sharpest throughout. When a member is addressing a problem or question to you, give him your undivided attention. Address your reply principally to him, but do not exclude the other board members.

8) Do not interrupt

A board member may be stating a problem for you to analyze. He will ask you a question when the time comes. Let him state the problem, and wait for the question.

9) Make sure you understand the question

Do not try to answer until you are sure what the question is. If it is not clear, restate it in your own words or ask the board member to clarify it for you. However, do not haggle about minor elements.

10) Reply promptly but not hastily

A common entry on oral board rating sheets is "candidate responded readily," or "candidate hesitated in replies." Respond as promptly and quickly as you can, but do not jump to a hasty, ill-considered answer.

11) Do not be peremptory in your answers

A brief answer is proper – but do not fire your answer back. That is a losing game from your point of view. The board member can probably ask questions much faster than you can answer them.

12) Do not try to create the answer you think the board member wants

He is interested in what kind of mind you have and how it works – not in playing games. Furthermore, he can usually spot this practice and will actually grade you down on it.

13) Do not switch sides in your reply merely to agree with a board member

Frequently, a member will take a contrary position merely to draw you out and to see if you are willing and able to defend your point of view. Do not start a debate, yet do not surrender a good position. If a position is worth taking, it is worth defending.

14) Do not be afraid to admit an error in judgment if you are shown to be wrong

The board knows that you are forced to reply without any opportunity for careful consideration. Your answer may be demonstrably wrong. If so, admit it and get on with the interview.

15) Do not dwell at length on your present job

The opening question may relate to your present assignment. Answer the question but do not go into an extended discussion. You are being examined for a *new* job, not your present one. As a matter of fact, try to phrase ALL your answers in terms of the job for which you are being examined.

Basis of Rating

Probably you will forget most of these "do's" and "don'ts" when you walk into the oral interview room. Even remembering them all will not ensure you a passing grade. Perhaps you did not have the qualifications in the first place. But remembering them will help you to put your best foot forward, without treading on the toes of the board members.

Rumor and popular opinion to the contrary notwithstanding, an oral board wants you to make the best appearance possible. They know you are under pressure – but they also want to see how you respond to it as a guide to what your reaction would be under the pressures of the job you seek. They will be influenced by the degree of poise you display, the personal traits you show and the manner in which you respond.

ABOUT THIS BOOK

This book contains tests divided into Examination Sections. Go through each test, answering every question in the margin. We have also attached a sample answer sheet at the back of the book that can be removed and used. At the end of each test look at the answer key and check your answers. On the ones you got wrong, look at the right answer choice and learn. Do not fill in the answers first. Do not memorize the questions and answers, but understand the answer and principles involved. On your test, the questions will likely be different from the samples. Questions are changed and new ones added. If you understand these past questions you should have success with any changes that arise. Tests may consist of several types of questions. We have additional books on each subject should more study be advisable or necessary for you. Finally, the more you study, the better prepared you will be. This book is intended to be the last thing you study before you walk into the examination room. Prior study of relevant texts is also recommended. NLC publishes some of these in our Fundamental Series. Knowledge and good sense are important factors in passing your exam. Good luck also helps. So now study this Passbook, absorb the material contained within and take that knowledge into the examination. Then do your best to pass that exam.

———

EXAMINATION SECTION

EXAMINATION SECTION
TEST 1

DIRECTIONS: Each question or incomplete statement is followed by several suggested answers or completions. Select the one the BEST answers the question or completes the statement. *PRINT THE LETTER OF THE CORRECT ANSWER IN THE SPACE AT THE RIGHT.*

1. The type of property/evidence that is most likely to involve the "two person" rule for handling is

   A. currency
   B. firearms
   C. flammable material
   D. biohazardous material

1.____

2. An affidavit is most likely to be required in a record for

   A. found property
   B. property seized by search warrant
   C. property held for safekeeping
   D. recovered property

2.____

3. "Temporary storage" refers to the

   A. gap between the time the employee who seized the property leaves it at the station, and the time that it is actually received by a property room employee
   B. gap between the time an item is signed out for disposition and the time that it is actually disposed of
   C. time during which non-evidentiary property is placed in the custody of a law enforcement agency for temporary protection on behalf of the owner
   D. span of any applicable statute of limitations that impacts the amount of time an item is required to remain in custody

3.____

4. When storing audio- or videotapes and computer disks, it's important to remember that air, heat, moisture, and magnetism may deteriorate these items within

   A. 6-8 months
   B. 1-2 years
   C. 5-6 years
   D. 10-12 years

4.____

5. A standard property/evidence record should include
   I.   date/time collected/submitted
   II. special instructions
   III. chain of custody
   IV. storage location

   A. I only
   B. I and III
   C. I, II and III
   D. I, II, III and IV

5.____

6. Biological materials must be in a sealed/container or bag   6.____

    A. if they are in transit
    B. only if they are to be used as evidence
    C. at all times
    D. if they are going to be tested again

7. Ideally, the outdoor "bulk area" of a property/evidence section would contain   7.____
    I. automobiles
    II. flammable materials
    III. firearms
    IV. bicycles

    A. I only
    B. I and IV
    C. I, II and IV
    D. I, II, III and IV

8. Materials and supplies used by the property/evidence section should be kept in the   8.____

    A. evidence review room
    B. general property/evidence storage area
    C. departmental office
    D. storage area separate from the entire section's facilities

9. Generally, inventories of property/evidence sections should be completed   9.____

    A. every three months
    B. every six months
    C. annually
    D. every two years

10. During an inventory, a property specialist comes across an item on the shelf that is not   10.____
documented anywhere in department records. The item should be listed on a(n)

    A. found property report
    B. disposition form
    C. unable to locate file
    D. right of refusal

11. When fingerprints on an item may be relevant and are a possibility, the item should be   11.____

    A. dusted for prints
    B. stored at room temperature
    C. frozen
    D. refrigerated

12. Guidelines for firearms storage include   12.____
    I. room should be alarmed independent of regular intrusion alarm system
    II. weapons should be secured in a manner that makes them impossible to fire
    III. weapons recovered from an underwater location should be cleaned
    IV. generally, firearms to be submitted for forensic processing should be packaged in an airtight container

A. I and II
B. II only
C. I, II and III
D. I, II, III and IV

13. What is the term for non-evidentiary property which, after coming into the custody of a law enforcement agency, has been determined to be lost or abandoned and is not known or suspected to be connected with any criminal offense?   13.____

   A. Property for safekeeping
   B. Found property
   C. Property for disposition
   D. Recovered property

14. Within a property/evidence section, narcotics which are most susceptible to theft from within the department are those which have   14.____

   A. just been signed off for disposition
   B. not yet been entered into evidence
   C. just been entered into evidence
   D. logged and stored indefinitely

15. Liquid items of biological samples, such as tubes of blood, that are meant to be tested again should be   15.____

   A. dried first, then stored at room temperature
   B. stored in refrigerator temperatures of 36-50 degrees Fahrenheit
   C. stored in freezer temperatures of below 32 degrees Fahrenheit
   D. vacuum-sealed, then stored at room temperature

16. For the handling, storage, and maintenance of high-profile items (narcotics, biological materials, firearms, currency, etc.), guidelines include each of the following, EXCEPT   16.____

   A. vaults should be constructed of concrete or block
   B. storage should be an exception to the overall property room location and scheme
   C. locking mechanisms should be designed so that two people are needed for entry
   D. alarm systems should consist of an intrusion alarm with door contacts and motion sensors

17. From the property specialist's standpoint, which of the following types of narcotics has different packaging requirements from most other kinds of drugs?   17.____

   A. partially processed methamphetamine
   B. cocaine
   C. green marijuana
   D. PCP

18. The original documentation of a property/evidence section inventory would be BEST kept   18.____

   A. with the records of the property/evidence section records
   B. with the agency's records bureau
   C. in a high-security area such as the firearms cabinet
   D. in the property supervisor/captain's office

19. Evidence stored with a property/evidence section may be disposed of if   19.____
    I.   it poses a physical hazard
    II. it is found property with unknown origins
    III. the case is subject to DA refiling
    IV. the case has multiple defendants

    A. I only
    B. I and III
    C. III only
    D. III and IV

20. Any property or evidence submitted to the property/evidence section should have an   20.____
    envelope, tag, or label affixed to it, usually corresponding with the _____ listed on the
    record.

    A. submitting officer
    B. case number
    C. classification
    D. item number

21. Which of the following is a guideline for the storage of computers?   21.____

    A. Disks and other storage media should be detached and stored separately.
    B. They should be stored in a covered outdoor bulk area.
    C. Towers should be stored in the position they were used in.
    D. They should be tightly sealed in metal containers.

22. Most appropriately, a departmental review of property/evidence for disposition would   22.____
    consist of

    A. basing disposition of statutes of limitations
    B. a complete inventory every 6 months-1 year
    C. a review of all criminal cases every 6 months-1 year
    D. an external audit of the efficiency with which space is being used

23. A standard currency envelope should contain each of the following, EXCEPT a   23.____

    A. space for witness verification
    B. space for the initials and the ID number of the person seizing and counting the cur-
       rency
    C. line for the name of additional owners/suspects whose cash is also included in the
       envelope
    D. register of currency and coins in the envelope, by denomination

24. Guidelines for recording and storing narcotics include   24.____
    I.   weights should be specified with (gross total weight) or without (net weight)
         packaging material
    II. after sealing the package, the only staff who should be authorized to re-open
         it are lab staff
    III. most narcotics should be stored in a heat-sealed plastic bag
    IV. scales used should be recalibrated at least twice a year

    A. I only
    B. I and II

C. I, II and IV
D. I, II, III and IV

25. It's important to note, prior to disposition, that _____ can be considered hazardous 25._____
waste because of the chemicals used to manufacture them.

A. television sets
B. computer circuit boards
C. computer hard drives
D. firearms

———

KEY (CORRECT ANSWERS)

1.	A		11.	B
2.	A		12.	A
3.	A		13.	B
4.	C		14.	A
5.	D		15.	B
6.	A		16.	B
7.	C		17.	C
8.	D		18.	B
9.	C		19.	A
10.	A		20.	D

21.	C
22.	C
23.	C
24.	D
25.	B

———

TEST 2

DIRECTIONS: Each question or incomplete statement is followed by several suggested answers or completions. Select the one the BEST answers the question or completes the statement. *PRINT THE LETTER OF THE CORRECT ANSWER IN THE SPACE AT THE RIGHT.*

1. The best method for marking a firearm is to attach an identification tag to the   1.____

   A. hammer
   B. checkered portion of the grip
   C. barrel
   D. trigger guard

2. "Chain of custody" of an item of evidence is usually considered to have been initiated by   2.____
   the

   A. property/evidence specialist
   B. original owner
   C. involved party
   D. recovering/reporting officer

3. Generally, the last item to appear on a standard property/evidence record is   3.____

   A. disposition
   B. involved party name
   C. storage location
   D. submitting officer/employee

4. The primary purpose of a property/evidence room inventory is to   4.____

   A. ensure continuity of custody
   B. provide quality control for departmental operations
   C. account for every single item of property
   D. streamline processes

5. The "Big Three" of in-custody property, which require extra protection, security, and han-   5.____
   dling precautions, include each of the following, EXCEPT

   A. firearms
   B. biohazardous materials
   C. narcotics
   D. currency

6. Probably the single most important factor in making the operation of a property/evidence   6.____
   section more efficient is

   A. commingling of different types of evidence in the same area
   B. packaging standards
   C. statutes of limitations
   D. transfer protocols

7. Bloody evidence, or evidence contaminated with other body fluids, should be dried in a   7.____
   controlled, secure environment. Once dried, the items are best stored in

A. airtight plastic
B. paper bags
C. the open air
D. tightly-wrapped foil

8. If not a separate department within a law enforcement agency, the property/evidence 8.____
function is most appropriately placed under the authority of

A. support services/administration
B. investigations division
C. property crimes division
D. uniform division

9. A submitting officer presents a sealed currency envelope to a property specialist without 9.____
an accompanying verification signature. The property specialist should

A. ask the officer to list the currency and coin by denomination
B. open the envelope and count the currency in order to provide corroboration
C. immediately transfer the currency to the general fund or finance department
D. exercise right of refusal

10. Containers used to store audio- or videotapes or computer disks should be each of the 10.____
following, EXCEPT

A. airtight
B. water-tight
C. metallic
D. non-static

11. Guidelines for conducting property/evidence section inventories include 11.____
   I. begin random inventories only from easy-to-describe locations
   II. if possible, conduct the inventory from paper to shelf
   III. if possible, avoid breaking evidence seals to verify contents
   IV. inventories of narcotics signed out for destruction should include random
      testing to determine purity

A. I only
B. I, III and IV
C. II and III
D. III and IV

12. When fireworks that have been stored with a property/evidence section are ready for dis- 12.____
posal, the most appropriate agency for the job is the

A. law enforcement agency that held them
B. Federal Bureau of Investigation
C. local fire department
D. federal ATF bureau

13. Guidelines for the storage of flammable materials include 13.____
   I. fire extinguishers or sprinkler systems should be available in the storage
      area
   II. storage in a metal container

III.   storage in an airtight container
IV.   if possible, storage outside the property room

A.   I only
B.   I and II
C.   I, II and III
D.   I, II, III and IV

14.   During an inventory, the seal on an envelope is broken. Which of the following is true?   14.____

A.   Any property contained within the envelope must now be destroyed.
B.   The contents must be verified and documented prior to resealing.
C.   The contents of the envelope are no longer admissible as evidence.
D.   The replacement seal does not require a witness.

15.   For narcotic evidence not taken into custody or destroyed at the scene, the recom-   15.____
mended documentation method is

A.   photographs taken prior to destruction
B.   small (.5 mg) samples taken and filed into envelopes
C.   an affidavit filed by the collecting officer and witnessed by the property specialist as
to the type and amount of substance
D.   a simple written description filed with property/evidence section records

16.   Unless disposal release is explicitly ordered, property/evidence from _____ should be   16.____
held indefinitely.
I.   falsification of public documents
II.   embezzlement of public funds
III.   felony sexual offenses
IV.   capital homicides

A.   I and II
B.   I, II and IV
C.   III and IV
D.   IV only

17.   To balance a desire to maximize a return on budgetary resources with the likelihood of   17.____
future obsolescence, a property/evidence section should keep a minimum of about
_____'s worth of forms (records, transfers, etc.) in stock.

A.   3 months
B.   6 months
C.   1 year
D.   3 years

18.   Which of the following is LEAST likely to be accepted into a property room as evidence   18.____
for storage?

A.   Bicycle
B.   Hypodermic syringe
C.   Currency
D.   Alcoholic beverage container

19. Bar coding systems, if used in a property/evidence records system, should allow for   19._____
      I.   password security
      II.   validation against the host system
      III.   on-demand label printing
      IV.   data collection programs for portable terminals

    A.   I and II
    B.   II only
    C.   II, III and IV
    D.   I, II, III and IV

20. The most efficient and trouble-free way to inventory a property/ evidence section is to   20._____

    A.   inventory different types of items at specific times of the year
    B.   work only from active case files
    C.   perform the inventory all at once at the beginning of each year
    D.   consult records only, without looking through individual items

21. When planning or adjusting the layout for a property/evidence storage area, it's important   21._____
to remember that property for safekeeping

    A.   should be commingled with non-quarantined evidence
    B.   requires its own separate ventilation system
    C.   needs quick, open access and close proximity to the public counter
    D.   should be placed on special shelving

22. The most significant factor influencing a property specialist's decision to dispose of prop-   22._____
erty or evidence is likely to be

    A.   civil litigation risk
    B.   auditing/inventory time
    C.   space limitations
    D.   increasing potential for misplacing items

23. Transfer forms used by property/evidence sections should NOT   23._____

    A.   include a brief description
    B.   indicate to whom the property was released
    C.   name the intended destination
    D.   be fastened to the original paperwork while in transit

24. Biological materials that are dried stains, and that are meant to be tested again, should   24._____
be stored

    A.   in the open air
    B.   in an airtight container at room temperature
    C.   in refrigerator temperatures of 36-50 degrees Fahrenheit
    D.   in freezer temperatures of below 32 degrees Fahrenheit

25. A law enforcement agency has discovered an item of found property in its storage facility,   25._____
and a quick search reveals the owner's identity. Which of the following may be true?
      I.   The law enforcement agency is not required to notify the owner.
      II.   The owner usually has 90 days after the receipt of the property by the
          agency to prove his ownership and reclaim the property.

III. The item has become the property of the law enforcement agency.
IV. The agency is authorized to require payment by the owner of a reasonable charge to defray the cost of storage and care of the property.

A. I and II
B. I, II and III
C. II and IV
D. I, II, III and IV

———————

KEY (CORRECT ANSWERS)

1.	D		11.	B
2.	D		12.	C
3.	A		13.	D
4.	A		14.	B
5.	B		15.	A
6.	B		16.	B
7.	B		17.	C
8.	A		18.	B
9.	D		19.	D
10.	C		20.	A

21. C
22. C
23. D
24. D
25. C

———————

EVALUATING INFORMATION AND EVIDENCE

SAMPLE QUESTIONS

These questions test for the ability to evaluate and draw conclusions from information and evidence. Each question consists of a set of facts and a conclusion based on the facts. You must decide if the conclusion is warranted by the facts.

TEST TASK: You will be given a set of FACTS and a CONCLUSION based on the facts. The conclusion is derived from these facts only — NOT on what you may happen to know about the subject discussed. Each question has three possible answers. You must then select the correct answer in the following manner:

Select A if the statements prove that the conclusion is TRUE.
Select B if the statements prove that the conclusion is FALSE.
Select C if the statements are INADEQUATE to prove the conclusion EITHER TRUE OR FALSE.

SAMPLE QUESTION #1

FACTS: All uniforms are cleaned by the Conroy Company. Blue uniforms are cleaned on Mondays or Fridays; green or brown uniforms are cleaned on Wednesdays. Alan and Jean have blue uniforms, Gary has green uniforms and Ryan has brown uniforms.

CONCLUSION: Jean's uniforms are cleaned on Wednesdays.
The correct answer to this sample question is B.

SOLUTION:
The last sentence of the FACTS says that Jean has blue uniforms. The second sentence of the FACTS says that blue uniforms are cleaned on Monday or Friday. The CONCLUSION says Jean's uniforms are cleaned on Wednesday. Wednesday is neither Monday nor Friday. Therefore, the conclusion must be FALSE (choice B).

SAMPLE QUESTION #2

FACTS: If Beth works overtime, the assignment will be completed. If the assignment is completed, then all unit employees will receive a bonus. Beth works overtime.

CONCLUSION: A bonus will be given to all employees in the unit.

The correct answer to this sample question is A.

SOLUTION:
The CONCLUSION follows necessarily from the FACTS. Beth works overtime. The assignment is completed. Therefore, all unit employees will receive a bonus.

SAMPLE QUESTION #3

FACTS: Bill is older than Wanda. Edna is older than Bill. Sarah is twice as old as Wanda.

CONCLUSION: Sarah is older than Edna.

The correct answer to this sample question is C.

SOLUTION:
We know from the facts that both Sarah and Edna are older than Wanda. We do not have any other information about Sarah and Edna. Therefore, no conclusion about whether or not Sarah is older than Edna can be made.

EVALUATING INFORMATION AND EVIDENCE
EXAMINATION SECTION
TEST 1

DIRECTIONS: Each question or incomplete statement is followed by several suggested answers or completions. Select the one that BEST answers the question or completes the statement. *PRINT THE LETTER OF THE CORRECT ANSWER IN THE SPACE AT THE RIGHT.*

Questions 1 -9

Questions 1 through 9 measure your ability to (1) determine whether statements from witnesses say essentially the same thing and (2) determine the evidence needed to make it reasonably certain that a particular conclusion is true.

1. Which of the following pairs of statements say essentially the same thing in two different ways?   1.____
   - I. Some employees at the water department have fully vested pensions.
         At least one employee at the water department has a pension that is not fully vested.
   - II. All swans are white birds.
         A bird that is not white is not a swan.

   A. I only
   B. I and II
   C. II only
   D. Neither I nor II

2. Which of the following pairs of statements say essentially the same thing in two different ways?   2.____
   - I. If you live in Humboldt County, your property taxes are high.
         If your property taxes are high, you live in Humboldt County.
   - II. All the Hutchinsons live in Lindsborg.
         At least some Hutchinsons do not live in Lindsborg.

   A. I only
   B. I and II
   C. II only
   D. Neither I nor II

3. Which of the following pairs of statements say essentially the same thing in two different ways?   3.____
   - I. Although Spike is a friendly dog, he is also one of the most unpopular dogs on the block.
         Although Spike is one of the most unpopular dogs on the block, he is a friendly dog.
   - II. Everyone in Precinct 19 is taller than Officer Banks.
         Nobody in Precinct 19 is shorter than Officer Banks.

   A. I only
   B. I and II
   C. II only
   D. Neither I nor II

4. Which of the following pairs of statements say essentially the same thing in two different ways?   4.___

    I. On Friday, every officer in Precinct 1 is assigned parking duty or crowd control, or both.
    If a Precinct 1 officer has been assigned neither parking duty nor crowd control, it is not Friday.

    II. Because the farmer mowed the hay fields today, his house will have mice tomorrow.
    Whenever the farmer mows his hay fields, his house has mice the next day.

    A. I only
    B. I and II
    C. II only
    D. Neither I nor II

5. Summary of Evidence Collected to Date: 5.___
    I. Fishing in the Little Pony River is against the law.
    II. Captain Rick caught an 8-inch trout and ate it for dinner.

Prematurely Drawn Conclusion: Captain Rick broke the law.

Which of the following pieces of evidence, if any, would make it *reasonably certain* that the conclusion drawn is true?

    A. Captain Rick caught his trout in the Little Pony River
    B. There is no size limit on trout mentioned in the law
    C. A trout is a species of fish
    D. None of these

6. Summary of Evidence Collected to Date: 6.___
    I. Some of the doctors in the ICU have been sued for malpractice
    II. Some of the doctors in the ICU are pediatricians

Prematurely Drawn Conclusion: Some of the pediatricians in the ICU have never been sued for malpractice

Which of the following pieces of evidence, if any, would make it *reasonably certain* that the conclusion drawn is true?

    A. The number of pediatricians in the ICU is the same as the number of doctors who have been sued for malpractice
    B. The number of pediatricians in the ICU is smaller than the number of doctors who have been sued for malpractice
    C. The number of ICU doctors who have been sued for malpractice is smaller than the number who are pediatricians
    D. None of these

7. Summary of Evidence Collected to Date: 7._____
    I.   Along Paseo Boulevard, there are five convenience stores
    II.   EZ-Go is east of Pop-a-Shop
    III.   Kwik-E-Mart is west of Bob's Market
    IV.   The Nightwatch is between EZ-Go and Kwik-E-Mart
Prematurely Drawn Conclusion: Pop-a-Shop is the westernmost convenience store on Paseo Boulevard

Which of the following pieces of evidence, if any, would make it *reasonably certain* that the conclusion drawn is true?

    A.   Bob's Market is the easternmost convenience store on Paseo
    B.   Kwik-E-Mart is the second store from the west
    C.   The Nightwatch is west of the EZ-Go
    D.   None of these

8. Summary of Evidence Collected to Date: 8._____
Stark drove home from work at 70 miles an hour and wasn't breaking the law
Prematurely Drawn Conclusion: Stark was either on an interstate highway or in the state of Montana
Which of the following pieces of evidence, if any, would make it *reasonably certain* that the conclusion drawn is true?

    A.   There are no interstate highways in Montana
    B.   Montana is the only state that allows a speed of 70 miles an hour on roads other than interstate highways
    C.   Most states don't allow speed of 70 miles an hour on state highways
    D.   None of these

9. Summary of Evidence Collected to Date: 9._____
    I.   Margaret, owner of *MetroWoman* magazine, signed a contract with each of her salespeople promising an automatic $200 bonus to any employee who sells more than 60 subscriptions in a calendar month
    II.   Lynn sold 82 subscriptions to *MetroWoman* in the month of December
Prematurely Drawn Conclusion: Lynn received a $200 bonus
Which of the following pieces of evidence, if any, would make it *reasonably certain* that the conclusion drawn is true?

    A.   Lynn is a salesperson
    B.   Lynn works for Margaret
    C.   Margaret offered only $200 regardless of the number of subscriptions sold
    D.   None of these

Questions 10-14

Questions 10 through 14 refer to Map #3 and measure your ability to orient yourself within a given section of town, neighborhood or particular area. Each of the questions describes a starting point and a destination. Assume that you are driving a car in the area shown on the map accompanying the questions. Use the map as a basis for the shortest way to get from one point to another without breaking the law.

On the map, a street marked by arrows, or by arrows and the words "One Way," indicates one-way travel, and should be assumed to be one-way for the entire length, even when there are breaks or jogs in the street. EXCEPTION: A street that does not have the same name over the full length.

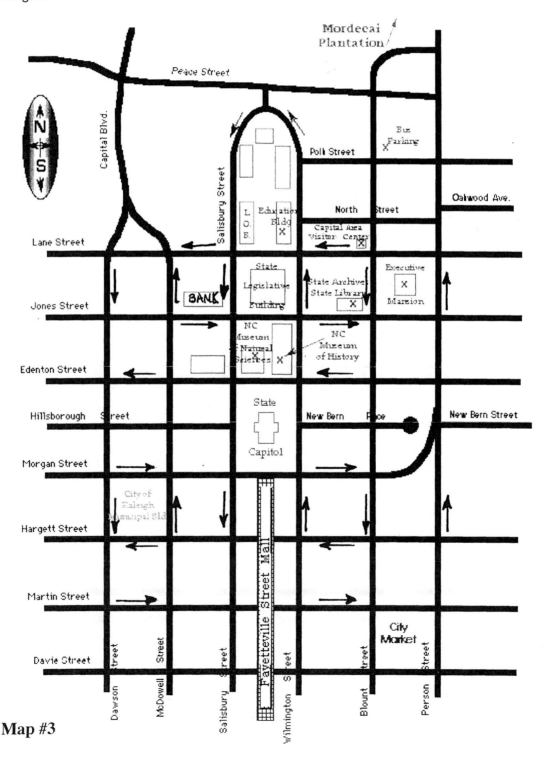

Map #3

10. The shortest legal way from the south end of the Fayetteville Street Mall, at Davie Street, to the city of Raleigh Municipal Building is 10._____

    A. west on Davie, north on McDowell
    B. west on Davie, north on Dawson
    C. east on Davie, north on Wilmington, west on Morgan
    D. east on Davie, north on Wilmington, west on Hargett

11. The shortest legal way from the City Market to the Education Building is 11._____

    A. north on Blount, west on North
    B. north on Person, west on Lane
    C. north on Blount, west on Lane
    D. west on Martin, north on Wilmington

12. The shortest legal way from the Education Building to the State Capitol is 12._____

    A. south on Wilmington
    B. north on Wilmington, west on Peace, south on Capitol, bear west to go south on Dawson, and east on Morgan
    C. west on Lane, south on Salisbury
    D. east on North, south on Blount, west on Edenton

13. The shortest legal way from the State Capitol to Peace College is 13._____

    A. north on Wilmington, jog north, east on Peace
    B. east on Morgan, north on Person, west on Peace
    C. west on Edenton, north on McDowell, north on Capitol Blvd., east on Peace
    D. east on Morgan, north on Blount, west on Peace

14. The shortest legal way from the State Legislative Building to the City Market is 14._____

    A. south on Wilmington, east on Martin
    B. east on Jones, south on Blount
    C. south on Salisbury, east on Davie
    D. east on Lane, south on Blount

Questions 15-19

Questions 15 through 19 refer to Figure #3, on the following page, and measure your ability to understand written descriptions of events. Each question presents a description of an accident or event and asks you which of the five drawings in Figure #3 BEST represents it.
In the drawings, the following symbols are used:

Moving vehicle: ⬠   Non-moving vehicle: ⬛

Pedestrian or bicyclist: ●

The path and direction of travel of a vehicle or pedestrian is indicated by a solid line.

The path and direction of travel of each vehicle or pedestrian directly involved in a collision from the point of impact is indicated by a dotted line.

In the space at the right, print the letter of the drawing that best fits the descriptions written below:

15. A driver headed north on Carson veers to the right and strikes a bicyclist who is also heading north. The bicyclist is thrown from the road. The driver flees north on Carson.   15.__

16. A driver heading south on Carson runs the stop sign and barely misses colliding with an eastbound cyclist. The cyclist swerves to avoid the collision and continues traveling east. The driver swerves to avoid the collision and strikes a car parked in the northbound lane on Carson.   16.__

17. A bicyclist heading west on Stone collides with a pedestrian in the crosswalk, then veers through the intersection and collides with the front of a car parked in the southbound lane on Carson.   17.__

18. A driver traveling south on Carson runs over a bicyclist who has run the stop sign, and then flees south on Carson.   18.__

19. A bicyclist heading west on Stone collides with the rear of a car parked in the westbound lane.   19.__

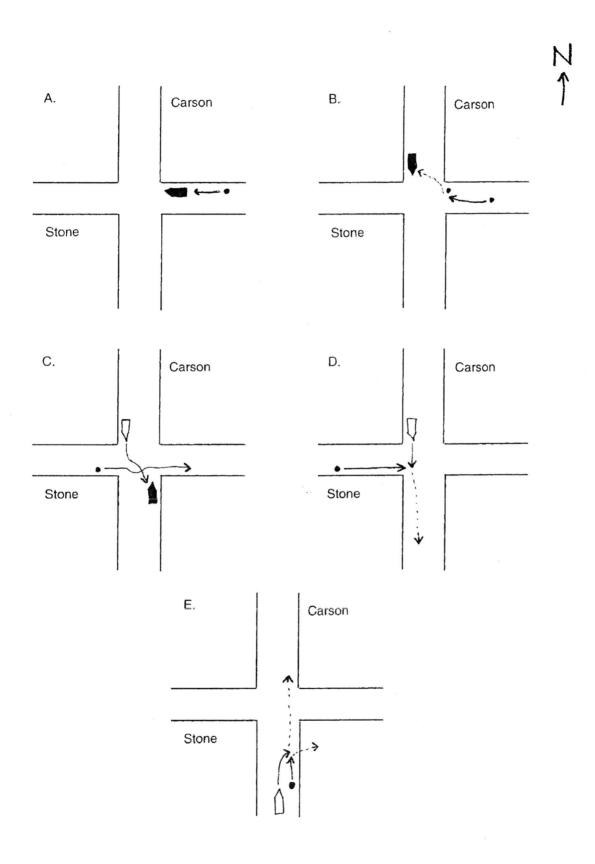

Questions 20-22

In questions 20 through 22, choose the word or phrase CLOSEST in meaning to the word or phrase printed in capital letters.

20. INSOLVENT   20.____

    A. bankrupt
    B. vagrant
    C. hazardous
    D. illegal

21. TENANT   21.____

    A. laborer
    B. occupant
    C. owner
    D. creditor

22. INFRACTION   22.____

    A. portion
    B. violation
    C. remark
    D. detour

Questions 23-25

Questions 23 through 25 measure your ability to do fieldwork-related arithmetic. Each question presents a separate arithmetic problem for you to solve.

23. Officer Jones has served on the police force longer than Smith. Smith has served longer   23.____
than Moore. Moore has served less time than Jones, and Park has served longer than
Jones.
Which officer has served the longest on the police force?

    A. Jones
    B. Smith
    C. Moore
    D. Park

24. A car wash has raised the price of an outside-only wash from $4 to $5. The car wash   24.____
applies the same percentage increase to its inside-and-out wash, which was $10. What
is the new cost of the inside-and-out wash?

    A. $8   B. $11   C. $12.50   D. $15

25. Ron and James, college students, make $10 an hour working at the restaurant. Ron   25.____
works 13 hours a week and James works 20 hours a week. To make the same amount
that Ron earns in a year, James would work about _____ weeks.

    A. 18   B. 27   C. 34   D. 45

KEY (CORRECT ANSWERS)

1.	C		11.	B
2.	D		12.	C
3.	B		13.	A
4.	B		14.	B
5.	A		15.	E
6.	D		16.	C
7.	B		17.	B
8.	B		18.	D
9.	B		19.	A
10.	A		20.	A

21.	B
22.	B
23.	D
24.	C
25.	C

————

SOLUTIONS TO QUESTIONS 1-9

P implies Q = original statement

Not Q implies not P = contrapositive of the original statement. A statement and its contrapositive are logically equivalent.

Q implies P = converse of the original statement.

Not P implies not Q = inverse of the original statement. The converse and inverse of an original statement are logically equivalent.

P implies Q = Not P or Q.

#1. The correct answer is **C**. Item I is wrong because "some employees" means "at least one employee" and possibly "all employees. If it is true that all employees have fully vested pensions, then the second statement is false. Item II is correct because the second statement is the contrapositive of the first statement.

#2. The correct answer is **D**. Item I is wrong because the converse of a statement does not necessarily follow from the original statement. Item II is wrong because statement I implies that there are no Hutchinson family members who live outside Lindsborg.

#3. The correct answer is **B**. Item I is correct because it is composed of the same two compound statements that are simply mentioned in a different order. Item II is correct because if each person is taller than Officer Banks, then there is no person in that precinct who can possibly be shorter than Officer Banks.

#4. The correct answer is **B**. Item I is correct because the second statement is the contrapositive of the first statement. Item II is correct because each statement indicates that mowing the hay fields on a particular day leads to the presence of mice the next day.

#5. The correct answer is **A**. If Captain Rick caught his trout in the Little Pony River, then we can conclude that he was fishing there. Since statement I says that fishing in the Little Pony River is against the law, we conclude that Captain Rick broke the law.

#6. The correct answer is **D**. The number of doctors in each group, whether the same or not, has no bearing on the conclusion. There is nothing in evidence to suggest that the group of doctors sued for malpractice overlaps with the group of doctors that are pediatricians.

#7. The correct answer is **B**. If we are given that Kwik-E-Mart is the second store from the west, then the order of stores, from west to east, is Pop-a - Shop, Kwik- E - Mart, Nightwatch, EZ- GO, and Bob's Market.

#8. The correct answer is **B**. We are given that Stark drove at 70 miles per hour and didn't break the law. If we also know that Montana is the only state that allows a speed of 70 miles per hour, then we can conclude that Stark must have been driving in Montana or else was driving on some interstate.

#9. The correct answer is **B**. The only additional piece of information needed is that Lynn works for Margaret. This will guarantee that Lynn receives the promised $200 bonus.

TEST 2

DIRECTIONS: Each question or incomplete statement is followed by several suggested answers or completions. Select the one that BEST answers the question or completes the statement. *PRINT THE LETTER OF THE CORRECT ANSWER IN THE SPACE AT THE RIGHT.*

Questions 1 -9

Questions 1 through 9 measure your ability to (1) determine whether statements from witnesses say essentially the same thing and (2) determine the evidence needed to make it reasonably certain that a particular conclusion is true.

To do well on this part of the test, you do NOT have to have a working knowledge of police procedures and techniques. Nor do you have to have any more familiarity with criminals and criminal behavior than that acquired from reading newspapers, listening to radio or watching TV. To do well in this part, you must read and reason carefully.

1. Which of the following pairs of statements say essentially the same thing in two different ways?
   I. All of the teachers at Slater Middle School are intelligent, but some are irrational thinkers.
       Although some teachers at Slater Middle School are irrational thinkers, all of them are intelligent.
   II. Nobody has no friends.
       Everybody has at least one friend.

   A. I only   B. I and II
   C. II only   D. Neither I nor II

1._____

2. Which of the following pairs of statements say essentially the same thing in two different ways?
   I. Although bananas taste good to most people, they are also a healthy food.
       Bananas are a healthy food, but most people eat them because they taste good.
   II. If Dr. Jones is in, we should call at the office.
       Either Dr. Jones is in, or we should not call at the office.

   A. I only   B. I and II
   C. II only   D. Neither I nor II

2._____

3. Which of the following pairs of statements say essentially the same thing in two different ways?
   I. Some millworkers work two shifts.
       If someone works only one shift, he is probably not a millworker.
   II. If a letter carrier clocks in at nine, he can finish his route by the end of the day.
       If a letter carrier does not clock in at nine, he cannot finish his route by the end of the day.

   A. I only   B. I and II
   C. II only   D. Neither I nor II

3._____

4. Which of the following pairs of statements say essentially the same thing in two different ways?

    I. If a member of the swim team attends every practice, he will compete in the next meet.
        Either a swim team member will compete in the next meet, or he did not attend every practice.

    II. All the engineers in the drafting department who wear glasses know how to use AutoCAD.
        If an engineer wears glasses he will know how to use AutoCAD.

    A. I only
    B. I and II
    C. II only
    D. Neither I nor II

4.___

5. Summary of Evidence Collected to Date:
All of the parents who attend the weekly parenting seminars are high school graduates.
Prematurely Drawn Conclusion: Some parents who attend the weekly parenting seminars have been convicted of child abuse.
Which of the following pieces of evidence, if any, would make it *reasonably certain* that the conclusion drawn is true?

    A. Those convicted of child abuse are often high school graduates
    B. Some high school graduates have been convicted of child abuse
    C. There is no correlation between education level and the incidence of child abuse
    D. None of these

5.___

6. Summary of Evidence Collected to Date:
    I. Mr. Cantwell promised to vote for new school buses if he was reelected to the board.
    II. If the new school buses are approved by the school board, then Mr. Cantwell was not reelected to the board.

Prematurely Drawn Conclusion: Approval of the new school buses was defeated in spite of Mr. Cantwell's vote.
Which of the following pieces of evidence, if any, would make it *reasonably certain* that the conclusion drawn is true?

    A. Mr. Cantwell decided not to run for reelection
    B. Mr. Cantwell was reelected to the board
    C. Mr. Cantwell changed his mind and voted against the new buses
    D. None of these

6.___

7.   <u>Summary of Evidence Collected to Date:</u>   7.____
      I.   The station employs three detectives: Francis, Jackson and Stern. One of the
         detectives is a lieutenant, one is a sergeant and one is a major.
     II.   Francis is not a lieutenant.
<u>Prematurely Drawn Conclusion:</u> Jackson is a lieutenant.
Which of the following pieces of evidence, if any, would make it *reasonably certain* that
the conclusion drawn is true?

   A.   Stern is not a sergeant
   B.   Stern is a major
   C.   Francis is a major
   D.   None of these

8.   <u>Summary of Evidence Collected to Date:</u>   8.____
      I.   In the office building, every survival kit that contains a gas mask also con-
         tains anthrax vaccine.
     II.   Some of the kits containing water purification tablets also contain anthrax
         vaccine.
<u>Prematurely Drawn Conclusion:</u> If the survival kit near the typists' pool contains a gas
mask, it does not contain water purification tablets.
Which of the following pieces of evidence, if any, would make it *reasonably certain* that
the conclusion drawn is true?

   A.   Some survival kits contain all three items
   B.   The survival kit near the typists' pool contains anthrax vaccine
   C.   The survival kit near the typists' pool contains only two of these items
   D.   None of these

9.   <u>Summary of Evidence Collected to Date:</u>   9.____
The shrink-wrap mechanism is designed to shut itself off if the heating coil temperature
drops below 400 during the twin cycle.
<u>Prematurely Drawn Conclusion:</u> If the machine was operating the twin cycle on Mon-
day, it was not operating properly.
Which of the following pieces of evidence, if any, would make it *reasonably certain* that
the conclusion drawn is true?

   A.   On Monday the heating coil temperature reached 450
   B.   When the machine performs functions other than the twin cycle, the heating coil
      temperature sometimes drops below 400
   C.   The shrink-wrap mechanism did not shut itself off on Monday
   D.   None of these

Questions 10-14

Questions 10 through 14 refer to Map #4, located on the following page, and measure your ability to orient yourself within a given section of town, neighborhood or particular area. Each of the
questions describes a starting point and a destination. Assume that you are driving a car in the
area shown on the map accompanying the questions. Use the map as a basis for the shortest
way to get from one point to another without breaking the law.

On the map, a street marked by arrows, or by arrows and the words "One Way," indicates one-way travel, and should be assumed to be one-way for the entire length, even when there are breaks or jogs in the street. EXCEPTION: A street that does not have the same name over the full length.

10. The shortest legal way from the State Capitol to Idaho Power is   10.____

     A. south on Capitol Blvd., west on Main, north on 12th
     B. south on 8th, west on Main
     C. west on Jefferson, south on 12th
     D. south on Capitol Blvd., west on Front, north on 12th

11. The shortest legal way from the Jefferson Place Building to the Statesman Building is   11.____

     A. east on Jefferson, south on Capitol Blvd.
     B. south on 8th, east on Main
     C. east on Jefferson, south on 4th, west on Main
     D. south on 9th, east on Main

12. The shortest legal way from Julia Davis Park to Owyhee Plaza Hotel is   12.____

     A. north on 5th, west on Front, north on 11th
     B. north on 6th, west on Main
     C. west on Battery, north on 9th, west on Front, north on Main
     D. north on 5th, west on Front, north on 13th, east on Main

13. The shortest legal way from the Big Easy to City Hall is   13.____

     A. north on 9th, east on Main
     B. east on Myrtle, north on Capitol Blvd.
     C. north on 9th, east on Idaho
     D. east on Myrtle, north on 6th

14. The shortest legal way from the Boise Contemporary Theater to the Pioneer Building is   14.____

     A. north on 9th, east on Main
     B. north on 9th, east on Myrtle, north on 6th
     C. east on Fulton, north on Capitol Blvd., east on Main
     D. east on Fulton, north on 6th

Downtown Districts

The Grove

The Capital District

Julia Davis Park/Cultural District

South Eighth Street Historic District

Old Boise Historic District

Central Downtown

Hotels

1 **The Grove Hotel**
   245 S. Capitol Blvd • (208) 333-8000

2 **The Statehouse Inn**
   981 W Grove St. • (208) 342-4622

3 **Best Western Safari Motor Inn**
   1070 W. Grove St. • (208) 344-9596

4 **Owyhee Plaza Hotel**
   1109 W. Main St • (208) 343-4611

Museums

1 Basque Museum

2 Idaho State Historical Museum

3 Black History Museum

4 Boise Art Museum

Points of Interest

1 Idaho Anne Frank Human Rights Memorial

2 Log Cabin Literary Center

3 Boise Public Library

4 Zoo Boise

5 Boise Contemporary Theater

6 Esther Simplot Performing Arts Center

7 Discovery Center

Parking

P Public Garages - First Hour Free

P Pay Lots/Garages

20 20 Minutes Free On All
    Downtown Parking Meters

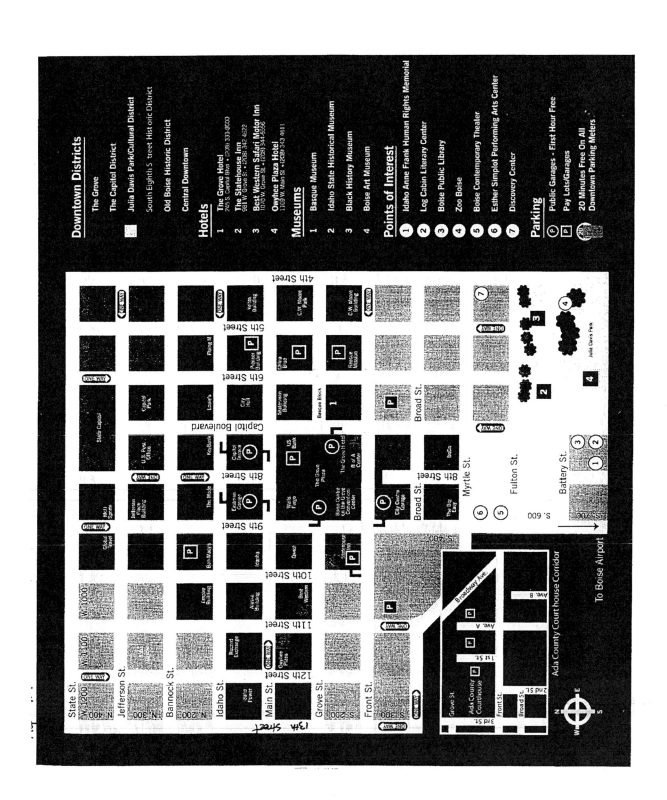

Questions 15-19

Questions 15 through 19 refer to Figure #4, on the following page, and measure your ability to understand written descriptions of events. Each question presents a description of an accident or event and asks you which of the five drawings in Figure #4 BEST represents it.

In the drawings, the following symbols are used:

Moving vehicle: ⬭   Non-moving vehicle: ⬛

Pedestrian or bicyclist: ●

The path and direction of travel of a vehicle or pedestrian is indicated by a solid line.

The path and direction of travel of each vehicle or pedestrian directly involved in a collision from the point of impact is indicated by a dotted line.

In the space at the right, print the letter of the drawing that best fits the descriptions written below:

15. A driver headed east on Union strikes a car that is pulling out from between two parked cars, and then continues east.   15.____

16. A driver headed north on Post strikes a car that is pulling out from in front of a parked car, then veers into the oncoming lane and collides head-on with a car that is parked in the southbound lane of Post.   16.____

17. A driver headed east on Union strikes a car that is pulling out from between two parked cars, travels through the intersection, and makes a sudden right turn onto Cherry, where he strikes a parked car in the rear.   17.____

18. A driver headed west on Union strikes a car that is pulling out from between two parked cars, and then swerves to the left. He cuts the corner and travels over the sidewalk at the intersection of Cherry and Post, and then strikes a car that is parked in the northbound lane on Post.   18.____

19. A driver headed east on Union strikes a car that is pulling out from between two parked cars, and then swerves to the left. He cuts the corner and travels over the sidewalk at the intersection of Oak and Post, and then flees north on Post.   19.____

FIGURE #4

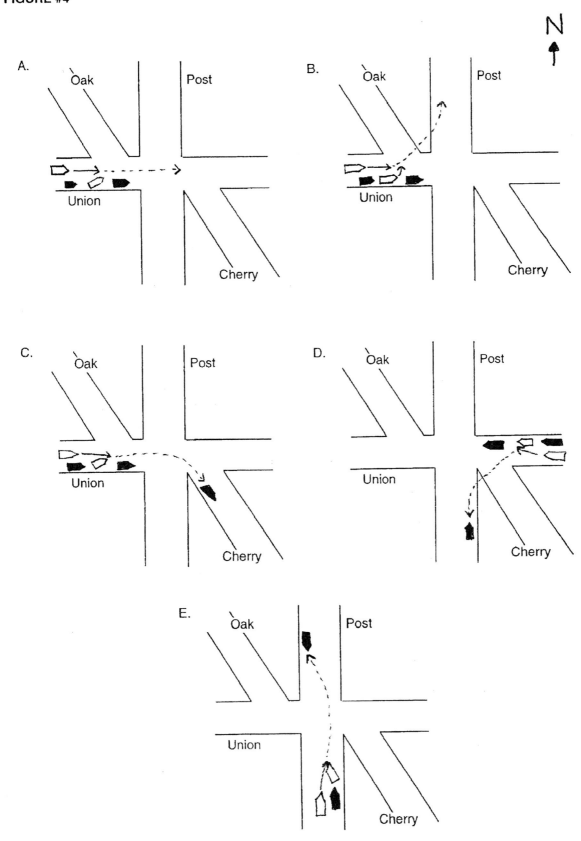

Questions 20-22

In questions 20 through 22, choose the word or phrase CLOSEST in meaning to the word or phrase printed in capital letters.

20. TITLE

    A. danger
    B. ownership
    C. description
    D. treatise

20.____

21. REVOKE

    A. cancel
    B. imagine
    C. solicit
    D. cause

21.____

22. BRIEF

    A. summary
    B. ruling
    C. plea
    D. motion

22.____

Questions 23-25

Questions 23 through 25 measure your ability to do fieldwork-related arithmetic. Each question presents a separate arithmetic problem for you to solve.

23. An investigator plans to drive from his home to Los Angeles, a trip of 2,800 miles. His car has a 24-gallon tank and gets 18 miles to the gallon. If he starts out with a full tank of gasoline, what is the FEWEST number of stops he will have to make for gasoline to complete his trip to Los Angeles?

    A. 4   B. 5   C. 6   D. 7

23.____

24. A caseworker has 24 home visits to schedule for a week. She will visit three homes on Sunday, and on every day that follows she will visit one more home than she visited on the previous day. At the end of the day on _____, the caseworker will have completed all of her home visits.

    A. Wednesday
    B. Thursday
    C. Friday
    D. Saturday

24.____

25. Ms. Langhorn takes a cab from her house to the airport. The cab company charges $3.00 to start the meter and $.50 per mile after that. It's 15 miles from Ms. Langhorn's house to the airport. How much will she have to pay for a cab?

    A. $10.50   B. $11.50   C. $14.00   D. $15.50

25.____

KEY (CORRECT ANSWERS)

1.	A		11.	D
2.	C		12.	A
3.	D		13.	B
4.	A		14.	C
5.	D		15.	A
6.	B		16.	E
7.	B		17.	C
8.	C		18.	D
9.	D		19.	B
10.	C		20.	B

21. A
22. A
23. C
24. B
25. A

SOLUTIONS TO QUESTIONS 1-9

P implies Q = original statement

Not Q implies not P = contrapositive of the original statement. A statement and its contrapositive are logically equivalent.

Q implies P = converse of the original statement.

Not P implies not Q = inverse of the original statement. The converse and inverse of an original statement are logically equivalent.

P implies Q = Not P or Q.

#1. The correct answer is **B**. For item I, the irrational thinking teachers at the Middle School belong the group of all Middle School teachers. Since all teachers at the Middle School are intelligent, this includes the subset of irrational thinkers. For item II, if no one person has no friends, this implies that each person must have at least one friend.

#2. The correct answer is **A**. In item I, both statements state that (a) bananas are healthy and (b) bananas are eaten mainly because they taste good. In item II, the second statement is not equivalent to the first statement. An equivalent statement to the first statement would be "Either Dr. Jones is not in or we should call at the office."

#3. The correct answer is **D**. In item I, given that a person works one shift, we cannot draw any conclusion about whether he/she is a millworker. It is possible that a millworker works one, two, or a number more than two shifts. In item II, the second statement is the inverse of the first statement; they are not logically equivalent.

#4. The correct answer is **B**. In item I, any statement in the form "P implies Q" is equivalent to "Not P or Q." In this case, P = A member of the swim team attends practice, and Q = He will compete in the next meet. In item II, "P implies Q" is equivalent to "all P belongs to Q." In this case, P = Engineer wears glasses, and Q = He will know how to use AutoCAD.

#5. The correct answer is **D**. Because the number of high school graduates is so much larger than the number of convicted child abusers, none of the additional pieces of evidence make it reasonably certain that there are convicted abusers within this group of parents.

#6. The correct answer is **B**. Statement II is equivalent to "If Mr. Cantwell is reelected to the school board, then school buses are not approved. Statement I assures us that Mr. Cantwell will vote for new school buses. The only logical conclusion is that in spite of Mr. Cantwell's reelection to the board and subsequent vote, approval of the buses was still defeated.

#7. The correct answer is **B**. From statement II, we conclude that Francis is either a sergeant or a major. If we also know that Stern is a major, we can deduce that Francis is a sergeant. This means that the third person, Jackson, must be a lieutenant.

#8. The correct answer is **C**. Given that a survival kit contains a gas mask, statement I assures us that it also contains the anthrax vaccine. If the survival kit near the typist pool only contains two items, then we can conclude that the gas mask in this location cannot contain a third item, namely the anthrax vaccine.

#9. The correct answer is **C**. The original statement can be written in "P implies Q" form, where P = The heating coil temperature drops below 400 during the twin cycle, and Q = The mechanism shuts itself off. The contrapositive (which must be true) would be " If the mechanism did not shut itself off, then the heating coil temperature did not drop below 400." We would then conclude that the temperature was too high and therefore the machine did not operate properly.

EXAMINATION SECTION
TEST 1

DIRECTIONS: Each question or incomplete statement is followed by several suggested answers or completions. Select the one that BEST answers the question or completes the statement. *PRINT THE LETTER OF THE CORRECT ANSWER IN THE SPACE AT THE RIGHT.*

Questions 1-6.

DIRECTIONS: Questions 1 through 6 are to be answered SOLELY on the basis of the numbered boxes on the Arrest Report and paragraph below.

ARREST REPORT

1.Arrest Number	2. Precinct of Arrest		3. Date/ Time of Arrest	4 .Defendant's Name		5. Defendant's Address
6.Defendant's Date of Birth	7. Sex	8. Race	9. Height	10. Weight	11. Location of Arrest	12. Date and Time of Occurrence
13. Location of Occurrence	14. Complaint Number		15. Victim's Name		16.Victim's Address	17. Victim's Date of Birth
18.Precinct of Complaint	19.Arresting Officer's Name		20. Shield Number		21.Assigned Unit Precinct	22.Date of Complaint

On Friday, December 13, at 11:45 P.M., while leaving a store at 235 Spring Street, Grace O'Connell, a white female, 5'2", 130 lbs., was approached by a white male, 5'11", 200 lbs., who demanded her money and jewelry. As the man ran and turned down River Street, Police Officer William James, Shield Number 31724, assigned to the 14th Precinct, gave chase and apprehended him in front of 523 River Street. The prisoner, Gerald Grande, who resides at 17 Water Street, was arrested at 12:05 A.M., was charged with robbery, and taken to the 13th Precinct, where he was assigned Arrest Number 53048. Miss O'Connell, who resides at 275 Spring St., was given Complaint Number 82460.

1. On the basis of the Arrest Report and paragraph above, the CORRECT entry for Box Number 3 should be   1.____

    A.   11:45 P.M., 12/13   B.   11:45 P.M., 12/14
    C.   12:05 A.M., 12/13   D.   12:05 A.M., 12/14

2. On the basis of the Arrest Report and paragraph above, the CORRECT entry for Box Number 21 should be

    A. 13th Precinct
    C. Mounted Unit

    B. 14th Precinct
    D. 32nd Precinct

2.____

3. On the basis of the Arrest Report and paragraph above, the CORRECT entry for Box Number 11 should be

    A. 235 Spring St.
    C. 275 Spring St.

    B. 523 River St.
    D. 17 Water St.

3.____

4. On the basis of the Arrest Report and paragraph above, the CORRECT entry for Box Number 2 should be

    A. 13th Precinct
    C. Mounted Unit

    B. 14th Precinct
    D. 32nd Precinct

4.____

5. On the basis of the Arrest Report and paragraph above, the CORRECT entry for Box Number 13 should be

    A. 523 River St.
    C. 275 Spring St.

    B. 17 Water St.
    D. 235 Spring St.

5.____

6. On the basis of the Arrest Report and paragraph above, the CORRECT entry for Box Number 14 should be

    A. 53048   B. 31724   C. 12/13   D. 82460

6.____

Questions 7-10.

DIRECTIONS: Questions 7 through 10 are to be answered SOLELY on the basis of the following information.

You are required to file various documents in file drawers which are labeled according to the following pattern:

DOCUMENTS

MEMOS		LETTERS	
File	Subject	File	Subject
84PM1 - (A-L)		84PC1 - (A-L)	
84PM2 - (M-Z)		84PC2 - (M-Z)	

REPORTS		INQUIRIES	
File	Subject	File	Subject
84PR1 - (A-L)		84PQ1 - (A-L)	
84PR2 - (M-Z)		84PQ2 - (M-Z)	

7. A letter dealing with a burglary should be filed in the drawer labeled

    A. 84PM1   B. 84PC1   C. 84PR1   D. 84PQ2

7.____

8. A report on *Statistics* should be found in the drawer labeled

    A. 84PM1   B. 84PC2   C. 84PR2   D. 84PQ2

8.____

9. An inquiry is received about parade permit procedures. It should be filed in the drawer   9.____
labeled

    A. 84PM2   B. 84PC1   C. 84PR1   D. 84PQ2

10. A police officer has a question about a robbery report you filed.   10.____
You should pull this file from the drawer labeled

    A. 84PM1   B. 84PM2   C. 84PR1   D. 84PR2

Questions 11-18.

DIRECTIONS: Questions 11 through 18 are to be answered SOLELY on the basis of the following information.
Below are listed the code number, name, and area of investigation of six detective units.

Each question describes a crime. For each question, choose the option (A, B, C, or D) which contains the code number for the detective unit responsible for handling that crime.

DETECTIVE UNITS

Unit Code No.	Unit Name	Unit's Area of Investigation
01	Senior Citizens Unit	All robberies of senior citizens 65 years or older
02	Major Case Unit	Any bank robbery; a commercial robbery where value of goods or money stolen is over $25,000
03	Robbery Unit	Any commercial, non-bank robbery where the value of the stolen goods or money is $25,000 or less; robberies of individuals under 65 years of age
04	Fraud and Larceny Unit	Confidence games and pickpockets
05	Special Investigations Unit	Burglaries of premises where the value of goods removed or monies taken is $15,000 or less
06	Burglary Unit	Burglaries of premises where the value of goods removed or monies taken is over $15,000

11. Mrs. Green calls the precinct and reports that her apartment was burglarized while she was on vacation and that precious jewelry and silverware, valued at $27,000, were taken. To which unit code number should her complaint be referred?

    A. 05   B. 02   C. 03   D. 06

11.___

12. Sylvia Bailey, Manager of the Building and Loan Savings Bank, reports that a man handed one of her tellers a note stating, *This is a robbery*. He had a gun and demanded money. The teller gave the man $500 in small bills, and the man then left. To which unit code number should the complaint be referred?

    A. 02   B. 06   C. 03   D. 05

12.___

13. Mrs. Miniver, a 67-year-old widow, states that she was beaten and robbed by two men in the elevator of her apartment building. To which unit code number should the complaint be referred?

    A. 06   B. 01   C. 03   D. 02

13.___

14. Mr. Whipple, Manager of T.V.A. Supermarket, reports that during the night someone entered the store and removed merchandise valued at $12,500. To which unit code number should the complaint be referred?

    A. 05   B. 03   C. 06   D. 02

14.___

15. Mr. Gold, owner of Gold's Jewelry Exchange, reports that two men, armed with shotguns, robbed his store and removed money and jewelry valued at $28,000. To which unit code number should the complaint be referred?

    A. 05   B. 03   C. 06   D. 02

15.___

16. Mr. Watson, a 62-year-old man, was walking in Central Park when he was approached by a man with a knife and was robbed of $72. To which unit code number should the complaint be referred?

    A. 01   B. 06   C. 03   D. 02

16.___

17. The Ace Jewelry Manufacturing Company was broken into over the weekend when the building was closed. The owner stated that $35,000 in gold, silver, diamonds, and jewelry were taken. To which unit code number should the complaint be referred?

    A. 02   B. 03   C. 06   D. 05

17.___

18. Mrs. Vargas, 62, reports that she gave Mr. Greene of the Starlite Realty Corporation $1,000 to locate a new apartment for her family. A week went by, and she never heard from Mr. Greene. She called the Starlite Realty Corporation, and they informed her that Mr. Greene never worked for Starlite Realty Corporation and that they have no record of the $1,000 deposit of Mrs. Vargas. To which unit code number should the complaint be referred?

    A. 04   B. 03   C. 01   D. 05

18.___

Questions 19-24.

DIRECTIONS: Questions 19 through 24 consist of sentences which contain examples of correct or incorrect English usage. Examine each sentence with reference to grammar, spelling, punctuation, and capitalization. Choose one of the following options that would be BEST for correct English usage:

    A. The sentence is correct.
    B. There is one mistake.
    C. There are two mistakes.
    D. There are three mistakes.

19. Mrs. Fitzgerald came to the 59th Precinct to retreive her property which were stolen earlier in the week.   19._____

20. The two officer's responded to the call, only to find that the perpatrator and the victim have left the scene.   20._____

21. Mr. Coleman called the 61st Precinct to report that, upon arriving at his store, he discovered that there was a large hole in the wall and that three boxes of radios were missing.   21._____

22. The Administrative Leiutenant of the 62nd Precinct held a meeting which was attended by all the civilians, assigned to the Precinct.   22._____

23. Three days after the robbery occured the detective apprahended two suspects and recovered the stolen items.   23._____

24. The Community Affairs Officer of the 64th Precinct is the liaison between the Precinct and the community; he works closely with various community organizations, and elected officials.   24._____

Questions 25-32.

DIRECTIONS: Questions 25 through 32 are to be answered on the basis of the following paragraph, which contains some deliberate errors in spelling and/or grammar and/or punctuation. Each line of the paragraph is preceded by a number. There are 9 lines and 9 numbers.

Line No.	Paragraph Line
1	The protection of life and proporty are, one of
2	the oldest and most important functions of a city.
3	New York city has it's own full-time police Agency.
4	The police Department has the power an it shall
5	be there duty to preserve the Public piece,
6	prevent crime detect and arrest offenders, supress
7	riots, protect the rites of persons and property, etc.
8	The maintainance of sound relations with the community they
9	serve is an important function of law enforcement officers.

25. How many errors are contained in line one? 25.___

    A. One   B. Two   C. Three   D. None

26. How many errors are contained in line two? 26.___

    A. One   B. Two   C. Three   D. None

27. How many errors are contained in line three? 27.___

    A. One   B. Two   C. Three   D. None

28. How many errors are contained in line four? 28.___

    A. One   B. Two   C. Three   D. None

29. How many errors are contained in line five? 29.___

    A. One   B. Two   C. Three   D. None

30. How many errors are contained in line six? 30.___

    A. One   B. Two   C. Three   D. None

31. How many errors are contained in line seven? 31.___

    A. One   B. Two   C. Three   D. None

32. How many errors are contained in line eight? 32.___

    A. One   B. Two   C. Three   D. None

Questions 33-40.

DIRECTIONS: Questions 33 through 40 are to be answered on the basis of the material con-tained in the INDEX OF CRIME IN CENTRAL CITY, U.S.A. 1994-2003 appear-ing on the following page. Certain information in various columns is deliberately left blank.

The correct answer (A, B, C, or D) to these questions requires you to make computations that will enable you to fill in the blanks correctly.

INDEX OF CRIME IN CENTRAL CITY, 1994-2003

	Crime Index Total	Violent Crime[1]	Property Crime[2]	Murder	Forcible Rape	Robbery	Aggra-vated Assault	Burglary	Larceny Theft	Motor Vehicle Theft
1994	8,717	875		19	51	385	420	2,565	4,347	930
1995	10,252	974	9,278	20	55	443	456		5,262	977
1996	11,256	1,026	10,230	20		465	485	3,253	5,977	1,000
1997	11,304	986		18	58	420	490	3,089	6,270	959
1998	10,935	1,009	9,926	19	63	405	522	3,053	5,905	968
1999	11,140	1,061	10,079	19	67	417	558	3,104	5,983	992
2000	12,152	1,178	10,974	23	75	466	614	3,299	6,578	1,097
2001	13,294	1,308	11,986	23	83		654	3,759	7,113	1,114
2002	13,289	1,321	11,968	22	82	574	643	3,740	7,154	1,074
2003	12,856	1,285	11,571	22	77	536	650	3,415	7,108	1,048

33. What was the TOTAL number of Property Crimes for 1994?　　　　33.____

    A.　9,740　　　　B.　10,252　　　　C.　16,559　　　　D.　7,842

34. What was the TOTAL number of Burglaries for 1995?　　　　34.____

    A.　2,062　　　　B.　3,039　　　　C.　3,259　　　　D.　4,001

35. In 2003, the total number of Aggravated Assaults was MOST NEARLY what percent of　　35.____
the total number of violent crimes for that year?

    A.　49.1　　　　B.　46.3　　　　C.　50.6　　　　D.　41.7

36. In 1998, Property Crime was MOST NEARLY what percent of the Crime Index Total?　　36.____

    A.　90.8　　　　B.　9.3　　　　C.　10.1　　　　D.　89.9

37. What was the TOTAL number of Property Crimes for 1997?　　　　37.____

    A.　10,318　　　　B.　11,304　　　　C.　986　　　　D.　10,808

38. What was the TOTAL number of Robberies for 2001?　　　　38.____

    A.　654　　　　B.　571　　　　C.　548　　　　D.　1,202

39. Robbery made up what percent of the TOTAL number of Violent Crimes for 2003?　　39.____

    A.　68.8%　　　　B.　4.1%　　　　C.　21.9%　　　　D.　41.7%

40. What was the TOTAL number of Forcible Rapes for 1996?　　　　40.____

    A.　47　　　　B.　56　　　　C.　55　　　　D.　101

KEY (CORRECT ANSWERS)

1.	D	11.	D	21.	A	31.	A
2.	B	12.	A	22.	C	32.	A
3.	B	13.	B	23.	C	33.	D
4.	A	14.	A	24.	B	34.	B
5.	D	15.	D	25.	C	35.	C
6.	D	16.	C	26.	D	36.	A
7.	B	17.	C	27.	C	37.	A
8.	C	18.	A	28.	B	38.	C
9.	D	19.	C	29.	C	39.	D
10.	D	20.	D	30.	B	40.	B

TEST 2

DIRECTIONS: Each question or incomplete statement is followed by several suggested answers or completions. Select the one that BEST answers the question or completes the statement. *PRINT THE LETTER OF THE CORRECT ANSWER IN THE SPACE AT THE RIGHT.*

Questions 1-8.

DIRECTIONS: Each of Questions 1 through 8 consists of three lines of code letters and numbers. The numbers on each line should correspond to the code letters on the same line in accordance with the table below.

Code Letter	X	B	L	T	V	M	P	F	J	S
Corresponding Number	0	1	2	3	4	5	6	7	8	9

On some of the lines, an error exists in the coding. Compare the letters and numbers in each question carefully. If you find an error or errors on:

Only <u>one</u> of the lines in the question, mark your answer A;
any <u>two</u> lines in the question, mark your answer B;
all <u>three</u> lines in the question, mark your answer C;
<u>none</u> of the lines in the question, mark your answer D.

<u>SAMPLE QUESTION</u>

MSXVLPT---5904263
SBFJLTP---9178246
XVMBTPF---8451367

In the above sample, the first line is correct since each code letter listed has the correct corresponding number. On the second line, an error exists because code letter T should have number 3 instead of number 4. On the third line, an error exists because the code letter X should have the number 0 instead of the number 8. Since there are errors on two of the three lines, the correct answer is B.

1. VFSTPLM---4793625
    SBXFLTP---9017236
    BTPJFSV---1358794

     1.___

2. TSLFVPJ---3927468
    JLFTVXS---8273409
    MVSXBFL---5490172

     2.___

3. XFTJSVT---0739843
    VFMTFLB---4753721
    LTFJSFM---2378985

     3.___

4. SJMSJVL---9859742
    VFBXMPF---3710568
    PFPXLBS---7670219

     4.___

5. MFPXVFP---5764076
    PTFJBLX---6378120
    VXSVSTB---4094931

     5.___

6. BXFPVJT---1076483
    STFMVLT---9375423
    TXPBTTM---3061335

    6._____

7. VLSBLVP---4290246
    FPSFBMV---7679154
    XTMXMLL---0730522

    7._____

8. JFVPMTJ---8746538
    TFPMXBL---3765012
    TJSFMFX---4987570

    8._____

Questions 9-18.

DIRECTIONS: Questions 9 through 1-8 each consists of two columns, each containing four lines of names, numbers and/or addresses. For each question, compare the lines in Column I with the lines in Column II to see if they match exactly, and mark your answer (A, B, C, or D) according to the following instructions:
  A. all four lines match exactly
  B. only three lines match exactly
  C. only two lines match exactly
  D. only one line matches exactly

9. (1) Earl Hodgson   Earl Hodgson   9._____
    (2) 1409870   1408970
    (3) Shore Ave.   Schore Ave.
    (4) Macon Rd.   Macon Rd.

10. (1) 9671485   9671485   10._____
    (2) 470 Astor Court   470 Astor Court
    (3) Halprin, Phillip   Halperin, Phillip
    (4) Frank D. Poliseo   Frank D. Poliseo

11. (1) Tandem Associates   –Tandom Associates   11._____
    (2) 144-17 Northern Blvd. 144-17 Northern Blvd.
    (3) Alberta Forchi   Albert Forchi
    (4) Kings Park, NY 10751 Kings Point, NY 10751

12. 1) Bertha C. McCormack   Bertha C. McCormack   12._____
    (2) Clayton, MO.   Clayton, MO.
    (3) 976-4242   976-4242
    (4) New City, NY 10951   New City, NY 10951

13. 1) George C. Morill   George C. Morrill   13._____
    (2) Columbia, SC 29201   Columbia, SD 29201
    (3) Louis Ingham   Louis Ingham
    (4) 3406 Forest Ave.   3406 Forest Ave.

14. (1) 506 S. Elliott Pl.   506 S. Elliott Pl.   14._____
    (2) Herbert Hall   Hurbert Hall
    (3) 4712 Rockaway Pkway   4712 Rockaway Pkway
    (4) 169 E. 7 St.   169 E. 7 St.

15. (1) 345 Park Ave.   345 Park Pl.   15._____
    (2) Colman Oven Corp.   Coleman Oven Corp.
    (3) Robert Conte   Robert Conti
    (4) 6179846   6179846

16. (1) Grigori Schierber   Grigori Schierber   16._____
    (2) Des Moines, Iowa   Des Moines, Iowa
    (3) Gouverneur Hospital   Gouverneur Hospital
    (4) 91-35 Cresskill Pl.   91-35 Cresskill Pl.

17. (1) Jeffery Janssen   Jeffrey Janssen   17._____
    (2) 8041071   8041071
    (3) 40 Rockefeller Plaza   40 Rockafeller Plaza
    (4) 407 6 St.   406 7 St.

18. (1) 5971996   5871996   18._____
    (2) 3113 Knickerbocker Ave. 3113 Knickerbocker Ave.
    (3) 8434 Boston Post Rd.   8424 Boston Post Rd.
    (4) Penn Station   Penn Station

Questions 19-22.

DIRECTIONS: Questions 19 through 22 are to be answered by looking at the 4 groups of names and addresses listed below (I, II, III, and IV) and then finding out the number of groups that have their corresponding numbered lines exactly the same.

	Group I	Group II
Line 1.	Ingersoll Public Library	Ingersoil Public Library
Line 2.	Reference and Research Dept.	Reference and Research Dept.
Line 3.	95-12 238 St.	95-12 238 St.
Line 4.	East Elmhurst, N.Y. 11357	East Elmhurst, N.Y. 11357

	Group III	Group IV
Line 1.	Ingersoll Public Library	Ingersoll Poblic Library
Line 2.	Reference and Research Dept.	Referance and Research Dept.
Line 3.	92-15 283 St.	95-12 283 St.
Line 4.	East Elmhurst, N.Y. 11357	East Elmhurst, N.Y. 11357

19. In how many groups is line one exactly the same?   19._____

    A. Two   B. Three   C. Four   D. None

20. In how many groups is line two exactly the same?   20._____

    A. Two   B. Three   C. Four   D. None

21. In how many groups is line three exactly the same?   21._____

    A. Two   B. Three   C. Four   D. None

22. In how many groups is line four exactly the same? 22.____

    A. Two   B. Three   C. Four   D. None

Questions 23-26.

DIRECTIONS: Questions 23 through 26 are to be answered by looking at the 4 groups of names and addresses listed below (I, II, III, and IV) and then finding out the number of groups that have their corresponding numbered lines exactly the same..

	Group I	Group II
Line 1.	Richmond General Hospital	Richman General Hospital
Line 2.	Geriatric Clinic	Geriatric Clinic
Line 3.	3975 Paerdegat St.	3975 Peardegat St.
Line 4.	Loudonville, New York 11538	Londonville, New York 11538

	Group III	Group IV
Line 1.	Richmond General Hospital	Richmend General Hospital
Line 2.	Geriatric Clinic	Geriatric Clinic
Line 3.	3795 Paerdegat St.	3975 Paerdegat St.
Line 4.	Loudonville, New York 11358	Loudonville, New York 11538

23. In how many groups is line one exactly the same? 23.____

    A. Two   B. Three   C. Four   D. None

24. In how many groups is line two exactly the same? 24.____

    A. Two   B. Three   C. Four   D. None

25. In how many groups is line three exactly the same? 25.____

    A. Two   B. Three   C. Four   D. None

26. In how many groups is line four exactly the same? 26.____

    A. Two   B. Three   C. Four   D. None

Questions 27-34.

DIRECTIONS: Each of Questions 27 through 34 consists of four or six numbered names. For each question, choose the option (A, B, C, or D) which indicates the order in which the names should be filed in accordance with the following filing instructions:

    - File alphabetically according to last name, then first name, then middle initial.
    - File according to each successive letter within a name.
    - When comparing two names where the letters in the longer name are identical with the corresponding letters in the shorter name, the shorter name is filed first.
    - When the last names are the same, initials are always filed before names beginning with the same letter.

27.   I. Ralph Robinson
           II. Alfred Ross
           III. Luis Robles
           IV. James Roberts

The CORRECT filing sequence for the above names should be

   A. IV, II, I, III   B. I, IV, III, II
   C. III, IV, I, II   D. IV, I, III, II

28.   I. Irwin Goodwin
           II. Inez Gonzalez
           III. Irene Goodman
           IV. Ira S. Goodwin
           V. Ruth I. Goldstein
           VI. M.B. Goodman

The CORRECT filing sequence for the above names should be

   A. V, II, I, IV, III, VI   B. V, II, VI, III, IV, I
   C. V, II, III, VI, IV, I   D. V, II, III, VI, I, IV

29.   I. George Allan
           II. Gregory Allen
           III. Gary Allen
           IV. George Allen

The CORRECT filing sequence for the above names should be

   A. IV, III, I, II   B. I, IV, II, III
   C. III, IV, I, II   D. I, III, IV, II

30.   I. Simon Kauffman
           II. Leo Kaufman
           III. Robert Kaufmann
           IV. Paul Kauffmann

The CORRECT filing sequence for the above names should be

   A. I, IV, II, III   B. II, IV, III, I
   C. III, II, IV, I   D. I, II, III, IV

31.   I. Roberta Williams
           II. Robin Wilson
           III. Roberta Wilson
           IV. Robin Williams

The CORRECT filing sequence for the above names should be

   A. III, II, IV, I   B. I, IV, III, II
   C. I, II, III, IV   D. III, I, II, IV

32.   I. Lawrence Shultz
           II. Albert Schultz
           III. Theodore Schwartz
           IV. Thomas Schwarz
           V. Alvin Schultz
           VI. Leonard Shultz

The CORRECT filing sequence for the above names should be

   A. II, V, III, IV, I, VI   B. IV, III, V, I, II, VI
   C. II, V, I, VI, III, IV   D. I, VI, II, V, III, IV

33.   I. McArdle   33.____

           II. Mayer

         III. Maletz

        IV. McNiff

         V. Meyer

       VI. MacMahon

The CORRECT filing sequence for the above names should be

  A. I, IV, VI, III, II, V   B. II, I, IV, VI, III, V
  C. VI, III, II, I, IV, V   D. VI, III, II, V, I, IV

34.   I. Jack E. Johnson   34.____

           II. R. H. Jackson

         III. Bertha Jackson

        IV. J. T. Johnson

         V. Ann Johns

       VI. John Jacobs

The CORRECT filing sequence for the above names should be

  A. II, III, VI, V, IV, I   B. III, II, VI, V, IV, I
  C. VI, II, III, I, V, IV   D. III, II, VI, IV, V, I

Questions 35-40.

DIRECTIONS: Questions 35 through 40 are to be answered SOLELY on the basis of the following passage.

An aide assigned to the Complaint Room must be familiar with the various forms used by that office. Some of these forms and their uses are:

Complaint Report	Used to record information on or information about crimes reported to the Police Department.
Complaint Report Follow-Up	Used to record additional information after the initial complaint report has been filed.
Aided Card	Used to record information pertaining to sick and injured persons aided by the police.
Accident Report	Used to record information on or information about injuries and/or property damage involving motorized vehicles.
Property Voucher	Used to record information on or information about property which comes into possession of the Police Department. (Motorized vehicles are not included.)
Auto Voucher	Used to record information on or information about a motorized vehicle which comes into possession of the Police Department.

35. Mr. Brown walks into the police precinct and informs the Administrative Aide that, while   35.____
he was at work, someone broke into his apartment and removed property belonging to him. He does not know everything that was taken, but he wants to make a report now and will make a list of what was taken and bring it in later.
According to the above passage, the CORRECT form to use in this situation should be the

  A. Property Voucher   B. Complaint Report
  C. Complaint Report Follow-Up   D. Aided Card

36. Mrs. Wilson telephones the precinct and informs the Administrative Aide she wishes to report additional property which was taken from her apartment. The Administrative Aide finds a Complaint Report had been previously filed for Mrs. Wilson.
According to the above passage, the CORRECT form to use in this situation should be the

    A. Property Voucher   B. Complaint Report
    C. Complaint Report Follow-Up   D. Aided Card

36.___

37. Police Officer Jones walks into the Complaint Room and informs the Administrative Aide that, while he was on patrol, he observed a woman fall to the sidewalk and remain there, apparently hurt. He comforted the injured woman and called for an ambulance, which came and brought the woman to the hospital.
According to the above passage, the CORRECT form on which to record this information should be the

    A. Accident Report   B. Complaint Report
    C. Complaint Report Follow-Up   D. Aided Card

37.___

38. Police Officer Smith informed the Administrative Aide assigned to the Complaint Room that Mr. Green, while crossing the street, was struck by a motorcycle and had to be taken to the hospital.
According to the above passage, the facts regarding this incident should be recorded on which one of the following forms?

    A. Accident Report   B. Complaint Report
    C. Complaint Report Follow-Up   D. Aided Card

38.___

39. Police Officer Williams reports to the Administrative Aide assigned to the Complaint Room that he and his partner, Police Officer Murphy, found an auto which was reported stolen and had the auto towed into the police garage.
Of the following forms listed in the above passage, which is the CORRECT one to use to record this information?

    A. Property Voucher   B. Auto Voucher
    C. Complaint Report Follow-Up   D. Complaint Report

39.___

40. Administrative Aide Lopez has been assigned to the Complaint Room. During her tour of duty, a person who does not identify herself hands Ms. Lopez a purse. The person states that she found the purse on the street. She then leaves the station house.
According to the information in the above passage, which is the CORRECT form to fill out to record the incident?

    A. Property Voucher   B. Auto Voucher
    C. Complaint Report Follow-Up   D. Complaint Report

40.___

KEY (CORRECT ANSWERS)

1.	B	11.	D	21.	A	31.	B
2.	D	12.	A	22.	C	32.	A
3.	B	13.	C	23.	A	33.	C
4.	C	14.	B	24.	C	34.	B
5.	A	15.	D	25.	A	35.	B
6.	D	16.	A	26.	A	36.	C
7.	C	17.	D	27.	D	37.	D
8.	A	18.	C	28.	C	38.	A
9.	C	19.	A	29.	D	39.	B
10.	B	20.	B	30.	A	40.	A

EXAMINATION SECTION
TEST 1

Questions 1-5.

DIRECTIONS: Each question from 1 to 5 consists of a sentence with an underlined word. For each question, select the choice that is *CLOSEST* in meaning to the underlined word.

EXAMPLE

This division reviews the <u>fiscal</u> reports of the agency.
In this sentence the word *fiscal* means most nearly
   A. financial   B. critical   C. basic   D. personnel
The correct answer is A. "financial" because "financial" is closest to *fiscal*. Therefore, the answer is A.

1. Every good office worker needs <u>basic</u> skills.   1.____
The word *basic* in this sentence means

   A. fundamental   B. advanced   C. unusual   D. outstanding

2. He turned out to be a good <u>instructor</u>.   2.____
The word *instructor* in this sentence means

   A. student   B. worker   C. typist   D. teacher

3. The <u>quantity</u> of work in the office was under study.   3.____
In this sentence, the word *quantity* means

   A. amount   B. flow   C. supervision   D. type

4. The morning was spent <u>examining</u> the time records.   4.____
In this sentence, the word *examining* means

   A. distributing   B. collecting   C. checking   D. filing

5. The candidate filled in the <u>proper</u> spaces on the form.   5.____
In this sentence, the word *proper* means

   A. blank   B. appropriate   C. many   D. remaining

Questions 6-8.

DIRECTIONS: You are to answer Questions 6 through 8 *SOLELY* on the basis of the information contained in the following paragraph:

The increase in the number of public documents in the last two centuries closely matches the increase in population in the United States. The great number of public documents has become a serious threat to their usefulness. It is necessary to have programs which will reduce the number of public documents that are kept and which will, at the same time, assure keeping those that have value. Such programs need a great deal of thought to have any success.

6. According to the above paragraph, public documents may be less useful if   6.____

    A. the files are open to the public
    B. the record room is too small
    C. the copying machine is operated only during normal working hours
    D. too many records are being kept

7. According to the above paragraph, the growth of the population in the United States has   7.____
matched the growth in the quantity of public documents for a period of, most nearly,

    A. 50 years   B. 100 years   C. 200 years   D. 300 years

8. According to the above paragraph, the increased number of public documents has made   8.____
it necessary to

    A. find out which public documents are worth keeping
    B. reduce the great number of public documents by decreasing government services
    C. eliminate the copying of all original public documents
    D. avoid all new copying devices.

Questions 9-10.

DIRECTIONS: You are to answer Questions 9 and 10 *SOLELY* on the basis of the information
contained in the following paragraph:
The work goals of an agency can best be reached if the employees understand and agree
with these goals. One way to gain such understanding and agreement is for management to
encourage and seriously consider suggestions from employees in the setting of agency goals.

9. On the basis of the paragraph above, the *BEST* way to achieve the work goals of an   9.____
agency is to

    A. make certain that employees work as hard as possible
    B. study the organizational structure of the agency
    C. encourage employees to think seriously about the agency's problems
    D. stimulate employee understanding of the work goals

10. On the basis of the paragraph above, understanding and agreement with agency goals   10.____
can be gained by

    A. allowing the employees to set agency goals
    B. reaching agency goals quickly
    C. legislative review of agency operations
    D. employee participation in setting agency goals

Questions 11-15.

DIRECTIONS: Each of Questions 11 through 15 consists of a group of four words. One word
in each group is *INCORRECTLY* spelled. For each question, print the letter of
the correct answer in the space at the right that is the same as the letter next
to the word which is *INCORRECTLY* spelled.
EXAMPLE
    A. housing   B. certain   C. budgit   D. money

The word "budgit" is incorrectly spelled, because the correct spelling should be "budget." Therefore, the correct answer is C.

11.	A. sentince	B. bulletin	C. notice	D. definition	11._____
12.	A. appointment	B. exactly	C. typest	D. light	12._____
13.	A. penalty	B. suparvise	C. consider	D. division	13._____
14.	A. schedule	B. accurate	C. corect	D. simple	14._____
15.	A. suggestion	B. installed	C. proper	D. agincy	15._____

Questions 16-20.

DIRECTIONS: Each question from 16 through 20 consists of a sentence which may be
- A. incorrect because of bad word usage, or
- B. incorrect because of bad punctuation, or
- C. incorrect because of bad spelling, or
- D. correct

Read each sentence carefully. Then print in the proper space at the right A, B, C, or D, according to the answer you choose from the four choices listed above. There is only one type of error in each incorrect sentence. If there is no error, the sentence is correct.

EXAMPLE

George Washington was the father of his contry.
This sentence is incorrect because of bad spelling ("contry" instead of "country"). Therefore, the answer is C.

16. The assignment was completed in record time but the payroll for it has not yet been pre-parid. 16._____

17. The operator, on the other hand, is willing to learn me how to use the mimeograph. 17._____

18. She is the prettiest of the three sisters. 18._____

19. She doesn't know; if the mail has arrived. 19._____

20. The doorknob of the office door is broke. 20._____

21. A clerk can process a form in 15 minutes. How many forms can that clerk process in six hours? 21._____

    A. 10   B. 21   C. 24   D. 90

22. An office staff consists of 120 people. Sixty of them have been assigned to a special project. Of the remaining staff, 20 answer the mail, 10-handle phone calls, and the rest operate the office machines. The number of people operating the office machines is 22._____

    A. 20   B. 30   C. 40   D. 45

23. An office worker received 65 applications but on the first day had to return 26 of them for being incomplete and on the second day 25 had to be returned for being incomplete. How many applications did <u>not</u> have to be returned? 23._____

    A. 10   B. 12   C. 14   D. 16

24. An office worker answered 63 phone calls in one day and 91 phone calls the next day. For these 2 days, what was the average number of phone calls he answered per day?

24.____

   A. 77   B. 28   C. 82   D. 93

25. An office worker processed 12 vouchers of $8.75 each, 3 vouchers of $3.68 each, and 2 vouchers of $1.29 each. The total dollar amount of these vouchers is

25.____

   A. $116.04   B. $117.52   C. $118.62   D. $119.04

———

KEY (CORRECT ANSWERS)

1. A		11. A	
2. D		12. C	
3. A		13. B	
4. C		14. C	
5. B		15. D	
6. D		16. C	
7. C		17. A	
8. A		18. D	
9. D		19. B	
10. D		20. A	

21. C
22. B
23. C
24. A
25. C

———

TEST 2

Questions 1-5.

EXAMPLE

Jensen, Alfred E.
Jensen, Alfred E.
Jensan, Alfred E.
Jensen, Fred E.

Since the name Jensen, Alfred E. appears twice and is exactly the same in both places, the correct answer is B.

1. Riviera, Pedro S.
   Rivers, Pedro S.
   Riviera, Pedro N.
   Riviera, Juan S.

   1.____

2. Guider, Albert
   Guidar, Albert
   Giuder, Alfred
   Guider, Albert

   2.____

3. Blum, Rona
   Blum, Rona
   Blum, Rona
   Blum, Rona

   3.____

4. Raugh, John
   Raugh, James
   Raughe, John
   Raugh, John

   4.____

5. Katz, Stanley
   Katz, Stanley
   Katze, Stanley
   Katz, Stanley

   5.____

Questions 6-10.

DIRECTIONS: Each Question 6 through 10 consists of numbers or letters in Columns I and II. For each question, compare each line of Column I with its corresponding line in Column II and decide how many lines in Column I are *EXACTLY* the same as their corresponding lines in Column II. In your answer space, mark your answer as follows:

Mark your answer A if only *ONE* line in Column I is exactly the same as its corresponding line in Column II
Mark your answer B if only *TWO* lines in Column I are exactly the same as their corresponding lines in Column II
Mark your answer C if only *THREE* lines in Column I are exactly the same as their corresponding lines in Column II
Mark your answer D if all *FOUR* lines in Column I are exactly the same as their corresponding lines in Column II

EXAMPLE

Column I	Column II
1776	1776
1865	1865
1945	1945
1976	1978

Only three lines in Column I are exactly the same as their corresponding lines in Column II. Therefore, the correct answer is C.

	Column I		Column II	
6.	5653		5653	6.__
	8727		8728	
	ZPSS		ZPSS	
	4952		9453	
7.	PNJP		PNPJ	7.__
	NJPJ		NJPJ	
	JNPN		JNPN	
	PNJP		PNPJ	
8.	effe		eFfe	8.__
	uWvw		uWvw	
	KpGj		KpGg	
	vmnv		vmnv	
9.	5232		5232	9.__
	PfrC		PfrN	
	zssz		zzss	
	rwwr		rwww	
10.	czws		czws	10.__
	cecc		cece	
	thrm		thrm	
	lwtz		lwtz	

Questions 11-15.

DIRECTIONS: Questions 11 through 15 have lines of letters and numbers. Each letter should be matched with its number in accordance with the following table:

Letter	F	R	C	A	W	L	E	N	B	T
Matching Number	0	1	2	3	4	5	6	7	8	9

From the table you can determine that the letter F has the matching number 0 below it, the letter R has the matching number 1 below it, etc.

For each question, compare each line of letters and numbers carefully to see if each letter has its correct matching number. If all the letters and numbers are matched correctly in

none of the lines of the question, mark your answer A

only *one* of the lines of the question, mark your answer B

only *two* of the lines of the question, mark your answer C

all three lines of the question, mark your answer D

EXAMPLE
WBCR	4826
TLBF	9580
ATNE	3986

There is a mistake in the first line because the letter R should have its matching number 1 instead of the number 6.

The second line is correct because each letter shown has the correct matching number.

There is a mistake in the third line because the letter N should have the matching number 7 instead of the number 8,

Since all the letters and numbers are matched correctly in only one of the lines in the sample, the correct answer is B.

11.   EBCT   6829   11._____
           ATWR   3961
           NLBW   7584

12.   RNCT   1729   12._____
           LNCR   5728
           WAEB   5368

13.   NTWB   7948   13._____
           RABL   1385
           TAEF   9360

14.   LWRB   5417   14._____
           RLWN   1647
           CBWA   2843

15.   ABTC   3792   15._____
           WCER   5261
           AWCN   3417

16. Your job often brings you into contact with the public. Of the following, it would be *MOST* desirable to explain the reasons for official actions to people coming into your office for assistance because such explanations

    A. help build greater understanding between the public and your agency
    B. help build greater self-confidence in city employees
    C. convince the public that nothing they do can upset a city employee
    D. show the public that city employees are intelligent

16.___

17. Assume that you strongly dislike one of your co-workers.
You should *FIRST*

    A. discuss your feeling with the co-worker
    B. demand a transfer to another office
    C. suggest to your supervisor that the co-worker should be observed carefully
    D. try to figure out the reason for this dislike before you say or do anything

17.___

18. An office worker who has problems accepting authority is *MOST* likely to find it difficult to

    A. obey rules   B. understand people
    C. assist other employees   D. follow complex instructions

18.___

19. The employees in your office have taken a dislike to one person and frequently annoy her. Your supervisor *should*

    A. transfer this person to another unit at the first opportunity
    B. try to find out the reason for the staff's attitude before doing anything about it
    C. threaten to transfer the first person observed bothering this person
    D. ignore the situation

19.___

20. Assume that your supervisor has asked a worker in your office to get a copy of a report out of the files. You notice the worker has accidentally pulled out the wrong report.
Of the following, the *BEST* way for you to handle this situation is to tell

    A. the worker about all the difficulties that will result from this error
    B. the worker about her mistake in a nice way
    C. the worker to ignore this error
    D. your supervisor that this worker needs more training in how to use the files

20.___

21. Filing systems differ in their efficiency. Which of the following is the *BEST* way to evaluate the efficiency of a filing system?
The

    A. number of times used per day
    B. amount of material that is received each day for filing
    C. amount of time it takes to locate material
    D. type of locking system used

21.___

22. In planning ahead so that a sufficient amount of general office supplies is always available, it would be *LEAST* important to find out the

    A. current office supply needs of the staff
    B. amount of office supplies used last year
    C. days and times that office supplies can be ordered
    D. agency goals and objectives

22.___

23. The *MAIN* reason for establishing routine office work procedures is that once a routine is established   23._____

    A. work need not be checked for accuracy
    B. all steps in the routine will take an equal amount of time to perform
    C. each time the job is repeated it will take less time to perform
    D. each step in the routine will not have to be planned all over again each time

24. When an office machine centrally located in an agency must be shut down for repairs, the bureaus and divisions using this machine should be informed of the   24._____

    A. expected length of time before the machine will be in operation again
    B. estimated cost of repairs
    C. efforts being made to avoid future repairs
    D. type of new equipment which the agency may buy in the future to replace the machine being repaired

25. If the day's work is properly scheduled, the *MOST* important result would be that the   25._____

    A. supervisor will not have to do much supervision
    B. employee will know what to do next
    C. employee will show greater initiative
    D. job will become routine

KEY (CORRECT ANSWERS)

1.	A		11.	C
2.	B		12.	B
3.	D		13.	D
4.	B		14.	B
5.	C		15.	A
6.	B		16.	A
7.	B		17.	D
8.	B		18.	A
9.	A		19.	B
10.	C		20.	B

21.	C
22.	D
23.	D
24.	A
25.	B

READING COMPREHENSION
UNDERSTANDING AND INTERPRETING WRITTEN MATERIAL
COMMENTARY

The ability to read, understand, and interpret written materials texts, publications, newspapers, orders, directions, expositions, legal passages is a skill basic to a functioning democracy and to an efficient business or viable government.

That is why almost all examinations – for beginning, middle, and senior levels – test reading comprehension, directly or indirectly.

The reading test measures how well you understand what you read. This is how it is done: You read a paragraph and several statements based on a question. From the statements, you choose the *one* statement, or answer, that is *BEST* supported by, or *BEST* matches, what is said in the paragraph.

SAMPLE QUESTIONS

DIRECTIONS: Each question has five suggested answers, lettered A, B, C, D, and E. Decide which one is the *BEST* answer. *PRINT THE LETTER OF THE CORRECT ANSWER IN THE SPACE AT THE RIGHT.*

1.   The prevention of accidents makes it necessary not only that safety devices be used to guard exposed machinery but also that mechanics be instructed in safety rules which they must follow for their own protection and that the light in the plant be adequate.
The paragraph BEST supports the statement that industrial accidents

    A.   are always avoidable
    B.   may be due to ignorance
    C.   usually result from inadequate machinery
    D.   cannot be entirely overcome
    E.   result in damage to machinery

ANALYSIS
Remember what you have to do -
    First   -   Read the paragraph.
    Second -   Decide what the paragraph means.
    Third   -   Read the five suggested answers.
    Fourth   -   Select the one answer which *BEST* matches what the paragraph says or is *BEST* supported by something in the paragraph. (Sometimes you may have to read the paragraph again in order to be sure which suggested answer is best.)

This paragraph is talking about three steps that should be taken to prevent industrial accidents:
    1.   use safety devices on machines
    2.   instruct mechanics in safety rules
    3.   provide adequate lighting

SELECTION

With this in mind, let's look at each suggested answer. Each one starts with "Industrial accidents ..."

SUGGESTED ANSWER A.

Industrial accidents (A) are always avoidable.

(The paragraph talks about how to avoid accidents but does not say that accidents are always avoidable.)

SUGGESTED ANSWER B.

Industrial accidents (B) may be due to ignorance.

(One of the steps given in the paragraph to prevent accidents is to instruct mechanics on safety rules. This suggests that lack of knowledge or ignorance of safety rules causes accidents. This suggested answer sounds like a good possibility for being the right answer.)

SUGGESTED ANSWER C.

Industrial accidents (C) usually result from inadequate machinery.

(The paragraph does suggest that exposed machines cause accidents, but it doesn't say that it is the usual cause of accidents. The word *usually* makes this a wrong answer.)

SUGGESTED ANSWER D.

Industrial accidents (D) cannot be entirely overcome.

(You may know from your own experience that this is a true statement. But that is not what the paragraph is talking about. Therefore, it is NOT the correct answer.)

SUGGESTED ANSWER E.

Industrial accidents (E) result in damage to machinery.

(This is a statement that may or may not be true, but, in any case, it is NOT covered by the paragraph.)

Looking back, you see that the one suggested answer of the five given that *BEST* matches what the paragraph says is

Industrial accidents (B) may be due to ignorance.
The *CORRECT* answer then is B.
Be sure you read *ALL* the possible answers before you make your choice. You may think that none of the five answers is really good, but choose the *BEST* one of the five.

---

2. Probably few people realize, as they drive on a concrete road, that steel is used to keep the surface flat in spite of the weight of the busses and trucks. Steel bars, deeply embedded in the concrete, provide sinews to take the stresses so that the stresses cannot crack the slab or make it wavy.
    The paragraph BEST supports the statement that a concrete road

A. is expensive to build
B. usually cracks under heavy weights
C. looks like any other road
D. is used only for heavy traffic
E. is reinforced with other material

ANALYSIS

This paragraph is commenting on the fact that -
1. few people realize, as they drive on a concrete road, that steel is deeply embedded
2. steel keeps the surface flat
3. steel bars enable the road to take the stresses without cracking or becoming wavy

SELECTION

Now read and think about the possible answers:
A. A concrete road is expensive to build.
   (Maybe so but that is not what the paragraph is about.)
B. A concrete road usually cracks under heavy weights.
   (The paragraph talks about using steel bars to prevent heavy weights from cracking concrete roads. It says nothing about how usual it is for the roads to crack. The word *usually* makes this suggested answer wrong.)
C. A concrete road looks like any other road.
   (This may or may not be true. The important thing to note is that it has nothing to do with what the paragraph is about.)
D. A concrete road is used only for heavy traffic.
   (This answer at least has something to do with the paragraph–concrete roads are used with heavy traffic but it does not say "used only.")
E. A concrete road is reinforced with other material.
   (This choice seems to be the correct one on two counts: *First,* the paragraph does suggest that concrete roads are made stronger by embedding steel bars in them. This is another way of saying "concrete roads are reinforced with steel bars." *Second,* by the process of elimination, the other four choices are ruled out as correct answers simply because they do not apply.)
You can be sure that not all the reading questions will be so easy as these.

────────────

SUGGESTIONS FOR ANSWERING READING QUESTIONS

1. Read the paragraph carefully. Then read each suggested answer carefully. Read every word, because often one word can make the difference between a right and a wrong answer.
2. Choose that answer which is supported in the paragraph itself. Do not choose an answer which is a correct statement unless it is based on information in the paragraph.
3. Even though a suggested answer has many of the words used in the paragraph, it may still be wrong.
4. Look out for words – such as *always, never, entirely, or only*–which tend to make a suggested answer wrong.

5. Answer first those questions which you can answer most easily. Then work on the other questions.
6. If you can't figure out the answer to the question, guess.

———

READING COMPREHENSION
UNDERSTANDING AND INTERPRETING WRITTEN MATERIAL
EXAMINATION SECTION
TEST 1

DIRECTIONS: The following questions are intended to test your ability to read with comprehension and to understand and interpret written materials, particularly legal
passages. It will be necessary for you to read each paragraph carefully because
the questions are based only on the material contained therein.
Each question has several suggested answers. *PRINT THE LETTER OF THE
CORRECT ANSWER IN THE SPACE AT THE RIGHT.*

Questions 1-3.

DIRECTIONS: Answer Questions 1 to 3 *SOLELY* on the basis of the following statement:
Foot patrol has some advantages over all other methods of patrol. Maximum opportunity
is provided for observation within range of the senses and for close contact with people and
things that enable the patrolman to provide a maximum service as an information source and
counselor to the public and as the eyes and ears of the police department. A foot patrolman
loses no time in alighting from a vehicle, and the performance of police tasks is not hampered
by responsibility for his vehicle while afoot. Foot patrol, however, does not have many of the
advantages of a patrol car. Lack of both mobility and immediate communication with headquarters lessens the officer's value in an emergency. The area that he can cover effectively is
limited and, therefore, this method of patrol is costly.

1. According to this paragraph, the foot patrolman is the eyes and ears of the police depart-   1.____
   ment because he is

   A. in direct contact with the station house
   B. not responsible for a patrol vehicle
   C. able to observe closely conditions on his patrol post
   D. a readily available information source to the public

2. The *MOST* accurate of the following statements concerning the various methods of   2.____
   patrol, according to this paragraph, is that

   A. foot patrol should sometimes be combined with motor patrol
   B. foot patrol is better than motor patrol
   C. helicopter patrol has the same advantages as motor patrol
   D. motor patrol is more readily able to communicate with superior officers in an emer-
      gency

3. According to this paragraph, it is *CORRECT* to state that foot patrol is   3.____

   A. *economical* since increased mobility makes more rapid action possible
   B. *expensive* since the area that can be patrolled is relatively small
   C. *economical* since vehicle costs need not be considered
   D. *expensive* since giving information to the public is time-consuming

Questions 4-6.

DIRECTIONS: Answer Questions 4 to 6 *SOLELY* on the basis of the following statement:
All applicants for an original license to operate a catering establishment shall be finger-printed. This shall include the officers, employees, and stockholders of the company and the members of a partnership. In case of a change, by addition or substitution, occurring during the existence of a license, the person added or substituted shall be fingerprinted. However, in the case of a hotel containing more than 200 rooms, only the officer or manager filing the application is required to be fingerprinted. The police commissioner may also at his discretion exempt the employees and stockholders of any company. The fingerprints shall be taken on one copy of form C.E. 20 and on two copies of C.E. 21. One copy of form C.E. 21 shall accompany the application. Fingerprints are not required with a renewal application.

4. According to this paragraph, an employee added to the payroll of a licensed catering establishment which is not in a hotel, must

    A. always be fingerprinted
    B. be fingerprinted unless he has been previously fingerprinted for another license
    C. be fingerprinted unless exempted by the police commissioner
    D. be fingerprinted only if he is the manager or an officer of the company

4.__

5. According to this paragraph, it would be *MOST* accurate to state that

    A. form C.E. 20 must accompany a renewal application
    B. form C.E. 21 must accompany all applications
    C. form C.E. 21 must accompany an original application
    D. both forms C.E. 20 and C.E. 21 must accompany all applications

5.__

6. A hotel of 270 rooms has applied for a license to operate a catering establishment on the premises. According to the instructions for fingerprinting given in this paragraph, the

    A. officers, employees, and stockholders shall be fingerprinted
    B. officers and manager shall be fingerprinted
    C. employees shall be fingerprinted
    D. officer filing the application shall be fingerprinted

6.__

Questions 7-9.

DIRECTIONS: Answer Questions 7 to 9 *SOLELY* on the basis of the following statement:
It is difficult to instill in young people inner controls on aggressive behavior in a world marked by aggression. The slum child's environment, full of hostility, stimulates him to delin-quency; he does that which he sees about him. The time to act against delinquency is before it is committed. It is clear that juvenile delinquency, especially when it is committed in groups or gangs, leads almost inevitably to an adult criminal life unless it is checked at once. The first signs of vandalism and disregard for the comfort, health, and property of the community should be considered as storm warnings which cannot be ignored. The delinquent's first crime has the underlying element of testing the law and its ability to hit back.

7. A *suitable* title for this entire paragraph based on the material it contains is: 7._____

    A. The Need for Early Prevention of Juvenile Delinquency
    B. Juvenile Delinquency as a Cause of Slums
    C. How Aggressive Behavior Prevents Juvenile Delinquency
    D. The Role of Gangs in Crime

8. According to this paragraph, an *INITIAL* act of juvenile crime *usually* involves a(n) 8._____

    A. group or gang activity
    B. theft of valuable property
    C. test of the strength of legal authority
    D. act of physical violence

9. According to this paragraph, acts of juvenile delinquency are *most likely* to lead to a crim- 9._____
inal career when they are

    A. acts of vandalism
    B. carried out by groups or gangs
    C. committed in a slum environment
    D. such as to impair the health of the neighborhood

Questions 10-12.

DIRECTIONS: Answer Questions 10 to 12 *SOLELY* on the basis of the following statement:
    The police laboratory performs a valuable service in crime investigation by assisting in
the reconstruction of criminal action and by aiding in the identification of persons and things.
When studied by a technician, physical things found at crime scenes often reveal facts useful
in identifying the criminal and in determining what has occurred. The nature of substances to
be examined and the character of the examinations to be made vary so widely that the services of a large variety of skilled scientific persons are needed in crime investigations. To
employ such a complete staff and to provide them with equipment and standards needed for
all possible analyses and comparisons is beyond the means and the needs of any but the
largest police departments. The search of crime scenes for physical evidence also calls for
the services of specialists supplied with essential equipment and assigned to each tour of
duty so as to provide service at any hour.

10. If a police department employs a large staff of technicians of various types in its labora- 10._____
tory, it will affect crime investigation to the extent that

    A. most crimes will be speedily solved
    B. identification of criminals will be aided
    C. search of crime scenes for physical evidence will become of less importance
    D. investigation by police officers will not usually be required

11. According to this paragraph, the *MOST* complete study of objects found at the scenes of 11._____
crimes is

    A. always done in all large police departments
    B. based on assigning one technician to each tour of duty
    C. probably done only in large police departments
    D. probably done in police departments of communities with low crime rates

12. According to this paragraph, a large variety of skilled technicians is useful in criminal investigations because   12.___

    A. crimes cannot be solved without their assistance as a part of the police team
    B. large police departments need large staffs
    C. many different kinds of tests on various substances can be made
    D. the police cannot predict what methods may be tried by wily criminals

Questions 13-14.

DIRECTIONS: Answer Questions 13 and 14 *SOLELY* on the basis of the following statement:
    The emotionally unstable person is always potentially a dangerous criminal, who causes untold misery to other persons and is a source of considerable trouble and annoyance to law enforcement officials. Like his fellow criminals he will be a menace to society as long as he is permitted to be at large. Police activities against him serve to sharpen his wits, and imprisonment gives him the opportunity to learn from others how to commit more serious crimes when he is released. This criminal's mental structure makes it impossible for him to profit by his experience with the police officials, by punishment of any kind or by sympathetic understanding and treatment by well-intentioned persons, professional and otherwise.

13. According to the above paragraph, the *MOST* accurate of the following statements concerning the relationship between emotional instability and crime is that   13.___

    A. emotional instability is proof of criminal activities
    B. the emotionally unstable person can become a criminal
    C. all dangerous criminals are emotionally unstable
    D. sympathetic understanding will prevent the emotionally unstable person from becoming a criminal

14. According to the above paragraph, the effect of police activities on the emotionally unstable criminal is that   14.___

    A. police activities aid this type of criminal to reform
    B. imprisonment tends to deter this type of criminal from committing future crimes
    C. contact with the police serves to assist sympathetic understanding and medical treatment
    D. police methods against this type of criminal develop him for further unlawful acts

Questions 15-17.

DIRECTIONS: Answer Questions 15 to 17 *SOLELY* on the basis of the following statement:
    Proposals to license gambling operations are based on the belief that the human desire to gamble cannot be suppressed and, therefore, it should be licensed and legalized with the people sharing in the profits, instead of allowing the underworld to benefit. If these proposals are sincere, then it is clear that only one is worthwhile at all. Legalized gambling should be completely controlled and operated by the state with all the profits used for its citizens. A state agency should be set up to operate and control the gambling business. It should be as completely removed from politics as possible. In view of the inherent nature of the gambling business, with its close relationship to lawlessness and crime, only a man of the highest integrity should be eligible to become head of this agency. However, state gambling would encourage mass gambling with its attending social and economic evils in the same manner as other forms of legal gambling; but there is no justification whatever for the business of gambling to be legalized and then permitted to operate for private profit or for the benefit of any political organization.

15. The *CENTRAL* thought of this paragraph may be *correctly* expressed as the   15._____

    A. need to legalize gambling in the state
    B. state operation of gambling for the benefit of the people
    C. need to license private gambling establishments
    D. evils of gambling

16. According to this paragraph, a problem of legalized gambling which will *still* occur if the   16._____
    state operates the gambling business is

    A. the diversion of profits from gambling to private use
    B. that the amount of gambling will tend to diminish
    C. the evil effects of any form of mass gambling
    D. the use of gambling revenues for illegal purposes

17. According to this paragraph, to legalize the business of gambling would be   17._____

    A. *justified* because gambling would be operated only by a man of the highest integrity
    B. *justified* because this would eliminate politics
    C. *unjustified* under any conditions because the human desire to gamble cannot be suppressed
    D. *unjustified* if operated for private or political profit

Questions 18-20.

DIRECTIONS: Answer Questions 18 to 20 *SOLELY* on the basis of the following statement:
    Whenever, in the course of the performance of their duties in an emergency, members of the force operate the emergency power switch at any location on the transit system and thereby remove power from portions of the track, or they are on the scene where this has been done, they will bear in mind that, although power is removed, further dangers exist; namely, that a train may coast into the area even though the power is off, or that the rails may be energized by a train which may be in a position to transfer electricity from a live portion of the third rail through its shoe beams. Employees must look in each direction before stepping upon, crossing, or standing close to tracks, being particularly careful not to come into contact with the third rail.

18. According to this paragraph, whenever an emergency occurs which has resulted in operating the emergency power switch, it is *MOST* accurate to state that   18._____

    A. power is shut off and employees may perform their duties in complete safety
    B. there may still be power in a portion of the third rail
    C. the switch will not operate if a portion of the track has been broken
    D. trains are not permitted to stop in the area of the emergency

19. An *important* precaution which this paragraph urges employees to follow after operating   19._____
    the emergency power switch, is to

    A. look carefully in both directions before stepping near the rails
    B. inspect the nearest train which has stopped to see if the power is on
    C. examine the third rail to see if the power is on
    D. check the emergency power switch to make sure it has operated properly

20. A trackman reports to you, a patrolman, that a dead body is lying on the road bed. You operate the emergency power switch. A train which has been approaching comes to a stop near the scene.
In order to act in accordance with the instructions in the above paragraph, you *should*

    A. climb down to the road bed and remove the body
    B. direct the train motorman to back up to the point where his train will not be in position to transfer electricity through its shoe beams
    C. carefully cross over the road bed to the body, avoiding the third rail and watching for train movements
    D. have the train motorman check to see if power is on before crossing to the tracks

20.___

21. The treatment to be given the offender cannot alter the fact of his offense; but we can take measures to reduce the chances of similar acts in the future. We should banish the criminal, not in order to exact revenge nor directly to encourage reform, but to deter him and others from further illegal attacks on society.
According to this paragraph, the *PRINCIPAL* reason for punishing criminals is to

    A. prevent the commission of future crimes
    B. remove them from society
    C. avenge society
    D. teach them that crime does not pay

21.___

22. Even the most comprehensive and best substantiated summaries of the total volume of criminal acts would not contribute greatly to an understanding of the varied social and biological factors which are sometimes assumed to enter into crime causation, nor would they indicate with any degree of precision the needs of police forces in combating crime.
According to this statement,

    A. crime statistics alone do not determine the needs of police forces in combating crime
    B. crime statistics are essential to a proper understanding of the social factors of crime
    C. social and biological factors which enter into crime causation have little bearing on police needs
    D. a knowledge of the social and biological factors of crime is essential to a proper understanding of crime statistics

22.___

23. The policeman's art consists of applying and enforcing a multitude of laws and ordinances in such degree or proportion and in such manner that the greatest degree of social protection will be secured. The degree of enforcement and the method of application will vary with each neighborhood and community.
According to the foregoing paragraph,

    A. each neighborhood or community must judge for itself to what extent the law is to be enforced
    B. a policeman should only enforce those laws which are designed to give the greatest degree of social protection
    C. the manner and intensity of law enforcement is not necessarily the same in all communities
    D. all laws and ordinances must be enforced in a community with the same degree of intensity

23.___

24. Police control in the sense of regulating the details of police operations, involves such matters as the technical means for so organizing the available personnel that competent police leadership, when secured, can operate effectively. It is concerned not so much with the extent to which popular controls can be trusted to guide and direct the course of police protection as with the administrative relationships which should exist between the component parts of the polie organism. According to the foregoing statement, police control is

24.____

   A. solely a matter of proper personnel assignment
   B. the means employed to guide and direct the course of police protection
   C. principally concerned with the administrative relationships between units of a police organization
   D. the sum total of means employed in rendering police protection

25. Police Department Rule 5 states that a Deputy Commissioner acting as Police Commissioner shall carry out the orders of the Police Commissioner, previously given, and such orders shall not, except in cases of extreme emergency, be countermanded. This means, most nearly, that, except in cases of extreme emergency,

25.____

   A. the orders given by a Deputy Commissioner acting as Police Commissioner may not be revoked
   B. a Deputy Commissioner acting as Police Commissioner should not revoke orders previously given by the Police Commissioner
   C. a Deputy Commissioner acting as Police Commissioner is vested with the same authority to issue orders as the Police Commissioner himself
   D. only a Deputy Commissioner acting as Police Commissioner may issue orders in the absence of the Police Commissioner himself

KEY (CORRECT ANSWERS)

1. C		11. C	
2. D		12. C	
3. B		13. B	
4. C		14. D	
5. C		15. B	
6. D		16. C	
7. A		17. D	
8. C		18. B	
9. B		19. A	
10. B		20. C	

21. A
22. A
23. C
24. C
25. B

TEST 2

Questions 1-2.

DIRECTIONS: Answer Questions 1 and 2 *SOLELY* on the basis of the following statement:
    The medical examiner may contribute valuable data to the investigator of fires which cause fatalities. By careful examination of the bodies of any victims, he not only establishes cause of death, but may also furnish, in many instances, answers to questions relating to the identity of the victim and the source and origin of the fire. The medical examiner is of greatest value to law enforcement agencies because he is able to determine the exact cause of death through an examination of tissue of apparent arson victims. Thorough study of a burned body or even of parts of a burned body will frequently yield information which illuminates the problems confronting the arson investigator and the police.

1. According to the above paragraph, the *MOST* important task of the medical examiner in the investigation of arson is to obtain information concerning the   1.__

    A. identity of arsonists   B. cause of death
    C. identity of victims   D. source and origin of fires

2. The *CENTRAL* thought of the above paragraph is that the medical examiner aids in the solution of crimes of arson when   2.__

    A. a person is burnt to death
    B. identity of the arsonist is unknown
    C. the cause of the fire is known
    D. trained investigators are not available

Questions 3-6.

DIRECTIONS: Answer Questions 3 to 6 *SOLELY* on the basis of the following statement:
    A foundling is an abandoned child whose identity is unknown. Desk officers shall direct the delivery, by a policewoman, if available, of foundlings actually or apparently under two years of age, to the Foundling Hospital, or if actually or apparently two years of age or over, to the Children's Center. In all other cases of dependent or neglected children, other than foundlings, requiring shelter, desk officers shall provide for obtaining such shelter as follows: between 9 a.m. and 5 p.m., Monday through Friday, by telephone direct to the Bureau of Child Welfare, in order to ascertain the shelter to which the child shall be sent; at all other times, direct the delivery of a child actually or apparently under two years of age to the Foundling Hospital, or, if the child is actually or apparently two years of age or over, to the Children's Center.

3. According to this paragraph, it would be *MOST* correct to state that   3.__

    A. a foundling as well as a neglected child may be delivered to the Foundling Hospital
    B. a foundling but not a neglected child may be delivered to the Children's Center
    C. a neglected child requiring shelter, regardless of age, may be delivered to the Bureau of Child Welfare
    D. the Bureau of Child Welfare may determine the shelter to which a foundling may be delivered

4. According to this paragraph, the desk officer shall provide for obtaining shelter for a neglected child, apparently under two years of age, by   4.____

    A. directing its delivery to the Children's Center if occurrence is on a Monday between 9 a.m. and 5 p.m.
    B. telephoning the Bureau of Child Welfare if occurrence is on a Sunday
    C. directing its delivery to the Foundling Hospital if occurrence is on a Wednesday at 4 p.m.
    D. telephoning the Bureau of Child Welfare if occurrence is at 10 a.m. on a Friday

5. According to this paragraph, the desk officer should direct delivery to the Foundling Hospital of any child who is   5.____

    A. actually under 2 years of age and requires shelter
    B. apparently under two years of age and is neglected or dependent
    C. actually 2 years of age and is a foundling
    D. apparently under 2 years of age and has been abandoned

6. A 12-year-old neglected child requiring shelter is brought to a police station on Thursday at 2 p.m. Such a child should be sent to   6.____

    A. a shelter selected by the Bureau of Child Welfare
    B. a shelter selected by the desk officer
    C. the Children's Center
    D. the Foundling Hospital when a brother or sister, under 2 years of age, also requires shelter

Questions 7-9.

DIRECTIONS: Answer Questions 7 to 9 *SOLELY* on the basis of the following statement:
    In addition to making the preliminary investigation of crimes, patrolmen should serve as eyes, ears, and legs for the detective division. The patrol division may be used for surveillance, to serve warrants and bring in suspects and witnesses, and to perform a number of routine tasks for the detectives which will increase the time available for tasks that require their special skills and facilities. It is to the advantage of individual detectives, as well as of the detective division, to have patrolmen working in this manner; more cases are cleared by arrest and a greater proportion of stolen property is recovered when, in addition to the detective regularly assigned, a number of patrolmen also work on the case. Detectives may stimulate the interest and participation of patrolmen by keeping them currently informed of the presence, identity, or description, hangouts, associates, vehicles and method of operation of each criminal known to be in the community.

7. According to this paragraph, a patrolman should   7.____

    A. assist the detective in certain of his routine functions
    B. be considered for assignment as a detective on the basis of his patrol performance
    C. leave the scene once a detective arrives
    D. perform as much of the detective's duties as time permits

8. According to this paragraph, patrolmen should aid detectives by   8.___

    A. accepting assignments from detectives which give promise of recovering stolen property

    B. making arrests of witnesses for the detective's interrogation

    C. performing all special investigative work for detectives

    D. producing for questioning individuals who may aid the detective in his investigation

9. According to this paragraph, detectives can keep patrolmen interested by   9.___

    A. ascertaining that patrolmen are doing investigative work properly

    B. having patrolmen directly under his supervision during an investigation

    C. informing patrolmen of the value of their efforts in crime prevention

    D. supplying the patrolmen with information regarding known criminals in the community

Questions 10-11.

DIRECTIONS: Answer Questions 10 and 11 *SOLELY* on the basis of the following statement:
State motor vehicle registration departments should and do play a vital role in the prevention and detection of automobile thefts. The combatting of theft is, in fact, one of the primary purposes of the registration of motor vehicles. As of recent date, there were approximately 61,309,000 motor vehicles registered in the United States. That same year some 200,000 of them were stolen. All but 6 percent have been or will be recovered. This is a very high recovery ratio compared to the percentage of recovery of other stolen personal property. The reason for this is that automobiles are carefully identified by the manufacturers and carefully registered by many of the states.

10. The *CENTRAL* thought of this paragraph is that there is a close relationship between the   10.___

    A. number of automobiles registered in the United States *and* the number stolen

    B. prevention of automobile thefts *and* the effectiveness of police departments in the United States

    C. recovery of stolen automobiles *and* automobile registration

    D. recovery of stolen automobiles *and* of other stolen property

11. According to this paragraph, the high recovery ratio for stolen automobiles is due to   11.___

    A. state registration and manufacturer identification of motor vehicles

    B. successful prevention of automobile thefts by state motor vehicle departments

    C. the fact that only 6% of stolen vehicles are not properly registered

    D. the high number of motor vehicles registered in the United States

Questions 12-15.

DIRECTIONS: Answer Questions 12 to 15 *SOLELY* on the basis of the following statement:
It is not always understood that the term "physical evidence" embraces any and all objects, living or inanimate. A knife, gun, signature, or burglar tool is immediately recognized as physical evidence. Less often is it considered that dust, microscopic fragments of all types, even an odor, may equally be physical evidence and often the most important of all. It is well established that the most useful types of physical evidence are generally microscopic in dimensions, that is, not noticeable by the eye and, therefore, most likely to be overlooked by

the criminal and by the investigator. For this reason, microscopic evidence persists for months or years after all other evidence has been removed and found inconclusive. Naturally, there are limitations to the time of collecting microscopic evidence as it may be lost or decayed. The exercise of judgment as to the possibility or profit of delayed action in collecting the evidence is a field in which the expert investigator should judge.

12. The *one* of the following which the above paragraph does *NOT* consider to be physical evidence is a   12._____

    A. criminal thought
    C. raw onion smell
    B. minute speck of dust
    D. typewritten note

13. According to the above paragraph, the re-checking of the scene of a crime   13._____

    A. is *useless* when performed years after the occurrence of the crime
    B. is *advisable* chiefly in crimes involving physical violence
    C. *may turn up* microscopic evidence of value
    D. *should be delayed* if the microscopic evidence is not subject to decay or loss

14. According to the above paragraph, the criminal investigator *should*   14._____

    A. give most of his attention to weapons used in the commission of the crime
    B. ignore microscopic evidence until a requiest is received from the laboratory
    C. immediately search for microscopic evidence and ignore the more visible objects
    D. realize that microscopic evidence can be easily overlooked

15. According to the above paragraph,   15._____

    A. a delay in collecting evidence must definitely diminish its value to the investigator
    B. microscopic evidence exists for longer periods of time than other physical evidence
    C. microscopic evidence is generally the most useful type of physical evidence
    D. physical evidence is likely to be overlooked by the criminal and by the investigator

Questions 16-18.

DIRECTIONS: Answer Questions 16 to 18 *SOLELY* on the basis of the following statement:
    Sometimes, but not always, firing a gun leaves a residue of nitrate particles on the hands. This fact is utilized in the paraffin test which consists of applying melted paraffin and gauze to the fingers, hands, and wrists of a suspect until a cast of approximately 1/8 of an inch is built up. The heat of the paraffin causes the pores of the skin to open and release any particles embedded in them. The paraffin cast is then removed and tested chemically for nitrate particles. In addition to gunpowder, fertilizers, tobacco ashes, matches,and soot are also common sources of nitrates on the hands.

16. Assume that the paraffin test has been given to a person suspected of firing a gun and that nitrate particles have been found. It would be *CORRECT* to conclude that the suspect   16._____

    A. is guilty
    C. may be guilty or innocent
    B. is innocent
    D. is probably guilty

17. In testing for the presence of gunpowder particles on human hands, the characteristic of paraffin which makes it *MOST* serviceable is that it
    A. causes the nitrate residue left by a fired gun to adhere to the gauze
    B. is waterproof
    C. melts at a low temperature
    D. helps to distinguish between gunpowder nitrates and other types

17.__

18. According to the above paragraph, in the paraffin test, the nitrate particles are removed from the pores because the paraffin
    A. enlarges the pores
    B. contracts the pores
    C. reacts chemically with nitrates
    D. dissolves the particles

18.__

Questions 19-21.

DIRECTIONS: Answer Questions 19 to 21 *SOLELY* on the basis of the following statement:
Pickpockets operate most effectively when there are prospective victims in either heavily congested areas or in lonely places. In heavily populated areas, the large number of people about them covers the activities of these thieves. In lonely spots, they have the advantage of working unobserved. The main factor in the pickpocket's success is the selection of the "right" victim, A pickpocket's victim must, at the time of the crime, be inattentive, distracted, or unconscious. If any of these conditions exist, and if the pickpocket is skilled in his operations, the stage is set for a successful larceny. With the coming of winter, the crowds move south-ward — and so do most of the pickpockets. However, some pickpockets will remain in certain areas all year around. They will concentrate on theater districts, bus and railroad terminals, hotels or large shopping centers. A complete knowledge of the methods of this type of criminal and the ability to recognize them come only from long years of experience in performing patient surveillance and trailing of them. This knowledge is essential for the effective control and apprehension of this type of thief.

19. According to this paragraph, the pickpocket is *LEAST* likely to operate in a

19.__

    A. baseball park with a full capacity attendance
    B. station in an outlying area late at night
    C. moderately crowded dance hall
    D. over-crowded department store

20. According to this paragraph, the one of the following factors which is *NOT* necessary for the successful operation of the pickpocket is that

20.__

    A. he be proficient in the operations required to pick pockets
    B. the "right" potential victims be those who have been the subject of such a theft pre-viously
    C. his operations be hidden from the view of others
    D. the potential victim be unaware of the actions of the pickpocket

21. According to this paragraph, it would be *MOST* correct to conclude that police officers who are successful in apprehending pickpockets

21.__

    A. are generalling those who have had lengthy experience in recognizing all types of criminals
    B. must, by intuition, be able to recognize potential "right" victims

C.   must follow the pickpockets in their southward movement
D.   must have acquired specific knowledge and skills in this field

Questions 22-23.

DIRECTIONS: Answer Questions 22 and 23 *SOLELY* on the basis of the following statement:
    For many years, slums had been recognized as breeding disease, juvenile delin-quency, and crime which not only threatened the health and welfare of the people who lived there, but also weakened the structure of society as a whole. As far back as 1834, a sanitary inspection report in the city pointed out the connection between insanitary, overcrowded housing and the spread of epidemics. Down through the years, evidence of slum-produced evils accumulated as the slums themselves continued to spread. This spread of slums was nationwide. Its symptoms and its ill effects were peculiar to no locality, but were characteristic of the country as a whole and imperiled the national welfare.

22.   According to this paragraph, people who live in slum dwellings   22._____

    A.   cause slums to become worse
    B.   are threatened by disease and crime
    C.   create bad housing
    D.   are the chief source of crime in the country

23.   According to this paragraph, the effects of juvenile delinquency and crime in slum areas were   23._____

    A.   to destroy the structure of society
    B.   noticeable in all parts of the country
    C.   a chief cause of the spread of slums
    D.   to spread insanitary conditions in the city

Questions 24-25.

DIRECTIONS: Questions 24 and 25 pertain to the following section of the Penal Law:
    Section 1942. A person who, after having been three times convicted within this state, of felonies or attempts to commit felonies, or under the law of any other state, government or country, of crimes which if committed within this state would be felonious, commits a felony, other than murder, first or second degree, or treason, within this state, shall be sentenced upon conviction of such fourth, or subsequent, offense to imprisonment in a state prison for an indeterminate term the minimum of which shall be not less than the maximum term pro-vided for first offenders for the crime for which the individual has been convicted, but, in any event, the minimum term upon conviction for a felony as the fourth, or subsequent, offense, shall be not less than fifteen years, and the maximum thereof shall be his natural life.

24.   Under the terms of the above stated portion of Section 1942 of the Penal Law, a person must receive the increased punishment therein provided *if*   24._____

    A.   he is convicted of a felony and has been three times previously convicted of felo-nies
    B.   he has been three times previously convicted of felonies, regardless of the nature of his present conviction

C.   his fourth conviction is for murder, first or second degree, or treason
D.   he has previously been convicted three times of murder, first or second degree, or treason

25.   Under the terms of the above stated portion of Section 1942 of the Penal Law, a person convicted of a felony for which the penalty is imprisonment for a term not to exceed ten years, and who has been three times previously convicted of felonies in this state, shall be sentenced to a term the *minimum* of which shall be

                                             25._____

    A.   ten years   B.   fifteen years
    C.   indeterminate   D.   his natural life

––––––––––

KEY (CORRECT ANSWERS)

1.	B		11.	A
2.	A		12.	A
3.	A		13.	C
4.	D		14.	D
5.	D		15.	C
6.	A		16.	C
7.	A		17.	A
8.	D		18.	A
9.	D		19.	C
10.	C		20.	B

21.	D
22.	B
23.	B
24.	A
25.	B

––––––––––

CLERICAL ABILITIES TEST

EXAMINATION SECTION
TEST 1

DIRECTIONS: Each question or incomplete statement is followed by several suggested answers or completions. Select the one that *BEST* answers the question or completes the statement. *PRINT THE LETTER OF THE CORRECT ANSWER IN THE SPACE AT THE RIGHT.*

Questions 1-10.

DIRECTIONS: Questions 1 through 10 consist of lines of names, dates and numbers. For each question, you are to choose the option (A, B, C, or D) in Column II which *EXACTLY* matches the information in Column I. *PRINT THE LETTER OF THE CORRECT ANSWER IN THE SPACE AT THE RIGHT.*

SAMPLE QUESTION

Column I	Column II		
Schneider 11/16/75 581932	A. Schneider	11/16/75	518932
	B. Schneider	11/16/75	581932
	C. Schnieder	11/16/75	581932
	D. Shnieder	11/16/75	518932

The correct answer is B. Only option B shows the name, date and number exactly as they are in Column I. Option A has a mistake in the number. Option C has a mistake in the name. Option D has a mistake in the name and in the number. Now answer Questions 1 through 10 in the same manner.

Column I	Column II

1. Johnston 12/26/74 659251
    A. Johnson 12/23/74 659251
    B. Johston 12/26/74 659251
    C. Johnston 12/26/74 695251
    D. Johnston 12/26/74 659251
    1._____

2. Allison 1/26/75 9939256
    A. Allison 1/26/75 9939256
    B. Alisson 1/26/75 9939256
    C. Allison 1/26/76 9399256
    D. Allison 1/26/75 9993256
    2._____

3. Farrell 2/12/75 361251
    A. Farell 2/21/75 361251
    B. Farrell 2/12/75 361251
    C. Farrell 2/21/75 361251
    D. Farrell 2/12/75 361151
    3._____

4. Guerrero 4/28/72 105689
    A. Guererro 4/28/72 105689
    B. Guererro 4/28/72 105986
    C. Guererro 4/28/72 105869
    D. Guerrero 4/28/72 105689
    4._____

5. McDonnell 6/05/73 478215

    A. McDonnell 6/15/73 478215
    B. McDonnell 6/05/73 478215
    C. McDonnell 6/05/73 472815
    D. MacDonell 6/05/73 478215

5.___

6. Shepard 3/31/71 075421

    A. Sheperd 3/31/71 075421
    B. Shepard 3/13/71 075421
    C. Shepard 3/31/71 075421
    D. Shepard 3/13/71 075241

6.___

7. Russell 4/01/69 031429

    A. Russell 4/01/69 031429
    B. Russell 4/10/69 034129
    C. Russell 4/10/69 031429
    D. Russell 4/01/69 034129

7.___

8. Phillips 10/16/68 961042

    A. Philipps 10/16/68 961042
    B. Phillips 10/16/68 960142
    C. Phillips 10/16/68 961042
    D. Philipps 10/16/68 916042

8.___

9. Campbell 11/21/72 624856

    A. Campbell 11/21/72 624856
    B. Campbell 11/21/72 624586
    C. Campbell 11/21/72 624686
    D. Campbel 11/21/72 624856

9.___

10. Patterson 9/18/71 76199176

    A. Patterson 9/18/72 76191976
    B. Patterson 9/18/71 76199176
    C. Patterson 9/18/72 76199176
    D. Patterson 9/18/71 76919176

10.___

Questions 11-15.

DIRECTIONS: Questions 11 through 15 consist of groups of numbers and letters which you are to compare. For each question, you are to choose the option (A, B, C, or D) in Column II which *EXACTLY* matches the group of numbers and letters given in Column I.

SAMPLE QUESTION

Column I	Column II
B92466	A. B92644
	B. B94266
	C. A92466
	D. B92466

The correct answer is D. Only option D in Column II shows the group of numbers and letters *EXACTLY* as it appears in Column I. Now answer Questions 11 through 15 in the same manner.

	Column I	Column II
11.	925AC5	A. 952CA5
		B. 925AC5
		C. 952AC5
		D. 925CA6

12. Y006925

A. Y060925
B. Y006295
C. Y006529
D. Y006925

13. J236956

A. J236956
B. J326965
C. J239656
D. J932656

14. AB6952

A. AB6952
B. AB9625
C. AB9652
D. AB6925

15. X259361

A. X529361
B. X259631
C. X523961
D. X259361

Questions 16-25.

DIRECTIONS: Each of Questions 16 through 25 consists of three lines of code letters and three lines of numbers. The numbers on each line should correspond with the code letters on the same line in accordance with the table below.

Code Letter	S	V	W	A	Q	M	X	E	G	K
Corresponding Number	0	1	2	3	4	5	6	7	8	9

On some of the lines, an error exists in the coding. Compare the letters and numbers in each question carefully. If you find an error or errors on:

only *one* of the lines in the question, mark your answer A;
any *two* lines in the question, mark your answer B;
all *three* lines in the question, mark your answer C;
none of the lines in the question, mark your answer D.

SAMPLE QUESTION

WQGKSXG   2489068
XEKVQMA   6591453
KMAESXV   9527061

In the above example, the first line is correct since each code letter listed has the correct corresponding number. On the second line, an error exists because code letter E should have the number 7 instead of the number 5. On the third line an error exists because the code letter A should have the number 3 instead of the number 2. Since there are errors in two of the three lines, the correct answer is B. Now answer Questions 16 through 25 in the same manner.

16. SWQEKGA   0247983   16._____
     KEAVSXM   9731065
     SSAXGKQ   0036894

17. QAMKMVS   4259510   17._____
     MGGEASX   5897306
     KSWMKWS   9125920

18.	WKXQWVE	2964217	18.____
	QKXXQVA	4966413	
	AWMXGVS	3253810	

19.	GMMKASE	8559307	19.____
	AWVSKSW	3210902	
	QAVSVGK	4310189	

20.	XGKQSMK	6894049	20.____
	QSVKEAS	4019730	
	GSMXKMV	8057951	

21.	AEKMWSG	3195208	21.____
	MKQSVQK	5940149	
	XGQAEVW	6843712	

22.	XGMKAVS	6858310	22.____
	SKMAWEQ	0953174	
	GVMEQSA	8167403	

23.	VQSKAVE	1489317	23.____
	WQGKAEM	2489375	
	MEGKAWQ	5689324	

24.	XMQVSKG	6541098	24.____
	QMEKEWS	4579720	
	KMEVKGA	9571983	

25.	GKVAMEW	8912572	25.____
	AXMVKAE	3651937	
	KWAGMAV	9238531	

Questions 26-35.

DIRECTIONS: Each of Questions 26 through 35 consists of a column of figures. For each question, add the column of figures and choose the correct answer from the four choices given.

26. 5,665.43   26.____
 2,356.69
 6,447.24
 7,239.65

   A. 20,698.01   B. 21,709.01
   C. 21,718.01   D. 22,609.01

27. 817,209.55   27.____
 264,354.29
  82,368.76
 849,964.89

   A. 1,893,997.49   B. 1,989,988.39
   C. 2,009,077.39   D. 2,013,897,49

28. 156,366.89
    249,973.23
    823,229.49
    <u>56,869.45</u>

    A. 1,286,439.06   B. 1,287,521.06
    C. 1,297,539.06   D. 1,296,421.06

28.____

29. 23,422.15
    149,696.24
    238,377.53
    86,289.79
    <u>505,544.63</u>

    A. 989,229.34   B. 999,879.34
    C. 1,003,330.34   D. 1,023,329.34

29.____

30. 2,468,926.70
    656,842.28
    49,723.15
    <u>832,369.59</u>

    A. 3,218,061.72   B. 3,808,092.72
    C. 4,007,861.72   D. 4,818,192.72

30.____

31. 524,201.52
    7,775,678.51
    8,345,299.63
    40,628,898.08
    <u>31,374,670.07</u>

    A. 88,646,647.81   B. 88,646,747.91
    C. 88,648,647.91   D. 88,648,747.81

31.____

32. 6,824,829.40
    682,482.94
    5,542,015.27
    775,678.51
    <u>7,732,507.25</u>

    A. 21,557,513.37   B. 21,567,513.37
    C. 22,567,503.37   D. 22,567,513.37

32.____

33. 22,109,405.58
    6,097,093.43
    5,050,073.99
    8,118,050.05
    <u>4,313,980.82</u>

    A. 45,688,593.87   B. 45,688,603.87
    C. 45,689,593.87   D. 45,689,603.87

33.____

34. 79,324,114.19
    99,848,129.74
    43,331,653.31
    <u>41,610,207.14</u>

34.____

A. 264,114,104.38   B. 264,114,114.38
C. 265,114,114.38   D. 265,214,104.38

35.   33,729,653.94
        5,959,342.58
     26,052,715.47
      4,452,669.52
      <u>7,079,953.59</u>

35.___

A. 76,374,334.10   B. 76,375,334.10
C. 77,274,335.10   D. 77,275,335.10

Questions 36-40.

DIRECTIONS: Each of Questions 36 through 40 consists of a single number in Column I and four options in Column II. For each question, you are to choose the option (A, B, C, or D) in Column II which *EXACTLY* matches the number in Column I.

SAMPLE QUESTION

<u>Column I</u>   <u>Column II</u>
5965121   A. 5956121
                      B. 5965121
                      C. 5966121
                      D. 5965211

The correct answer is B. Only option B shows the number *EXACTLY* as it appears in Column I. Now answer Questions 36 through 40 in the same manner.

<u>Column I</u>		<u>Column II</u>
36.	9643242	A. 9643242
		B. 9462342
		C. 9642442
		D. 9463242
37.	3572477	A. 3752477
		B. 3725477
		C. 3572477
		D. 3574277
38.	5276101	A. 5267101
		B. 5726011
		C. 5271601
		D. 5276101
39.	4469329	A. 4496329
		B. 4469329
		C. 4496239
		D. 4469239
40.	2326308	A. 2236308
		B. 2233608
		C. 2326308
		D. 2323608

KEY (CORRECT ANSWERS)

1.	D	11.	B	21.	A	31.	D
2.	A	12.	D	22.	C	32.	A
3.	B	13.	A	23.	B	33.	B
4.	D	14.	A	24.	D	34.	A
5.	B	15.	D	25.	A	35.	C
6.	C	16.	D	26.	B	36.	A
7.	A	17.	C	27.	D	37.	C
8.	C	18.	A	28.	A	38.	D
9.	A	19.	D	29.	C	39.	B
10.	B	20.	B	30.	C	40.	C

TEST 2

Questions 1-5.

DIRECTIONS: Each of Questions 1 through 5 consists of a name and a dollar amount. In each question, the name and dollar amount in Column II should be an exact copy of the name and dollar amount in Column I. If there is:

a mistake only in the name, mark your answer A;

a mistake only in the dollar amount, mark your answer B;

a mistake in both the name and the dollar amount, mark your answer C;

no mistake in either the name or the dollar amount, mark your answer D.

SAMPLE QUESTION

Column I	Column II
George Peterson	George Petersson
$125.50	$125.50

Compare the name and dollar amount in Column II with the name and dollar amount in Column I. The name *Petersson* in Column II is spelled *Peterson* in Column I. The amount is the same in both columns. Since there is a mistake only in the name, the answer to the sample question is A.

Now answer Questions 1 through 5 in the same manner.

Column I	Column II	
1. Susanne Shultz $3440	Susanne Schultz $3440	1.___
2. Anibal P. Contrucci $2121.61	Anibel P. Contrucci $2112.61	2.___
3. Eugenio Mendoza $12.45	Eugenio Mendozza $12.45	3.___
4. Maurice Gluckstadt $4297	Maurice Gluckstadt $4297	4.___
5. John Pampellonne $4656.94	John Pammpellonne $4566.94	5.___

Questions 6-11.

DIRECTIONS: Each of Questions 6 through 11 consists of a set of names and addresses which you are to compare. In each question, the name and addresses in Column II should be an *EXACT* copy of the name and address in Column I. If there is:

a mistake only in the name, mark your answer A;

a mistake only in the address, mark your answer B;

a mistake in both the name and address, mark your answer C;

no mistake in either the name or address, mark your answer D.

SAMPLE QUESTION

Column I	Column II
Michael Filbert	Michael Filbert
456 Reade Street	645 Reade Street
New York, N.	New York, N . Y. 10013

Since there is a mistake only in the address (the street number should be 456 instead of 645), the answer to the sample question is B.

Now answer Questions 6 through 11 in the same manner.

Column I	Column II	
6. Hilda Goettelmann 55 Lenox Rd. Brooklyn, N. Y. 11226	Hilda Goetteleman 55 Lenox Ave. Brooklyn, N. Y. 11226	6._____
7. Arthur Sherman 2522 Batchelder St. Brooklyn, N. Y. 11235	Arthur Sharman 2522 Batcheder St. Brooklyn, N. Y. 11253	7._____
8. Ralph Barnett 300 West 28 Street New York, New York 10001	Ralph Barnett 300 West 28 Street New York, New York 10001	8._____
9. George Goodwin 135 Palmer Avenue Staten Island, New York 10302	George Godwin 135 Palmer Avenue Staten Island, New York 10302	9._____
10. Alonso Ramirez 232 West 79 Street New York, N. Y. 10024	Alonso Ramirez 223 West 79 Street New York, N. Y. 10024	10._____
11. Cynthia Graham 149-35 83 Street Howard Beach, N. Y. 11414	Cynthia Graham 149-35 83 Street Howard Beach, N. Y. 11414	11._____

Questions 12-20.

DIRECTIONS: Questions 12 through 20 are problems in subtraction. For each question do the subtraction and select your answer from the four choices given.

12. 232,921.85
    -179,587.68   12._____

    A. 52,433.17   B. 52,434.17
    C. 53,334.17   D. 53,343.17

13. 5,531,876.29
    -3,897,158.36   13._____

    A. 1,634,717.93   B. 1,644,718.93
    C. 1,734,717.93   D. 1,734,718.93

14. 1,482,658.22
    - 937,925.76   14._____

    A. 544,633.46   B. 544,732.46
    C. 545,632.46   D. 545,732.46

15. 937,828.17
    -259,673.88   15._____

    A. 678,154.29   B. 679,154.29
    C. 688,155.39   D. 699,155.39

16. 760,412.38
    -263,465.95   16.

    A. 496,046.43   B. 496,946.43
    C. 496,956.43   D. 497,046.43

17. 3,203,902.26
    -2,933,087.96   17.

    A. 260,814.30   B. 269,824.30
    C. 270,814.30   D. 270,824.30

18. 1,023,468.71
    - 934,678.88   18.

    A. 88,780.83   B. 88,789.83
    C. 88,880.83   D. 88,889.83

19. 831,549.47
    -772,814.78   19.

    A. 58,734.69   B. 58,834.69
    C. 59,735,69   D. 59,834.69

20. 6,306,281.74
    -3,617,376.75   20.

    A. 2,687,904.99   B. 2,688,904.99
    C. 2,689,804.99   D. 2,799,905.99

Questions 21-30.

DIRECTIONS: Each of Questions 21 through 30 consists of three lines of code letters and three lines of numbers. The numbers on each line should correspond with the code letters on the same line in accordance with the table below.

Code Letter	J	U	B	T	Y	D	K	R	L	P
Corresponding Number	0	1	2	3	4	5	6	7	8	9

On some of the lines, an error exists in the coding. Compare the letters and numbers in each question carefully. If you find an error or errors on:

    only *one* of the lines in the question, mark your answer A;
    any *two* lines in the question, mark your answer B;
    all *three* lines in the question, mark your answer C;
    none of the lines in the question, mark your answer D.

SAMPLE QUESTION

    BJRPYUR   2079417
    DTBPYKJ   5328460
    YKLDBLT   4685283

In the above sample the first line is correct since each code letter listed has the correct corresponding number. On the second line, an error exists because code letter P should have the number 9 instead of the number 8. The third line is correct since each code letter listed has the correct corresponding number. Since there is an error in *one* of the three lines, the correct answer is A.

Now answer Questions 21 through 30 in the same manner.

21.	BYPDTJL	2495308	21.____
	PLRDTJU	9815301	
	DTJRYLK	5207486	
22.	RPBYRJK	7934706	22.____
	PKTYLBU	9624821	
	KDLPJYR	6489047	
23.	TPYBUJR	3942107	23.____
	BYRKPTU	2476931	
	DUKPYDL	5169458	
24.	KBYDLPL	6345898	24.____
	BLRKBRU	2876261	
	JTULDYB	0318542	
25.	LDPYDKR	8594567	25.____
	BDKDRJL	2565708	
	BDRPLUJ	2679810	
26.	PLRLBPU	9858291	26.____
	LPYKRDJ	8936750	
	TDKPDTR	3569527	
27.	RKURPBY	7617924	27.____
	RYUKPTJ	7426930	
	RTKPTJD	7369305	
28.	DYKPBJT	5469203	28.____
	KLPJBTL	6890238	
	TKPLBJP	3698209	
29.	BTPRJYL	2397148	29.____
	LDKUTYR	8561347	
	YDBLRPJ	4528190	
30.	ULPBKYT	1892643	30.____
	KPDTRBJ	6953720	
	YLKJPTB	4860932	

KEY (CORRECT ANSWERS)

1.	A		16.	B
2.	C		17.	C
3.	A		18.	B
4.	D		19.	A
5.	C		20.	B
6.	C		21.	B
7.	C		22.	C
8.	D		23.	D
9.	A		24.	B
10.	B		25.	A
11.	D		26.	C
12.	C		27.	A
13.	A		28.	D
14.	B		29.	B
15.	A		30.	D

CLERICAL ABILITIES

EXAMINATION SECTION
TEST 1

DIRECTIONS: Each question or incomplete statement is followed by several suggested answers or completions. Select the one that BEST answers the question or completes the statement. *PRINT THE LETTER OF THE CORRECT ANSWER IN THE SPACE AT THE RIGHT.*

Questions 1-4.

DIRECTIONS: Questions 1 through 4 are to be answered on the basis of the information given below.

The most commonly used filing system and the one that is easiest to learn is alphabetical filing. This involves putting records in an A to Z order, according to the letters of the alphabet. The name of a person is filed by using the following order: first, the surname or last name; second, the first name; third, the middle name or middle initial. For example, *Henry C. Young* is filed under *Y* and thereafter under *Young, Henry C.* The name of a company is filed in the same way. For example, *Long Cabinet Co.* is filed under *L,* while *John T. Long Cabinet Co.* is filed under *L* and thereafter under *Long., John T. Cabinet Co.*

1. The one of the following which lists the names of persons in the CORRECT alphabetical order is:

    A. Mary Carrie, Helen Carrol, James Carson, John Carter
    B. James Carson, Mary Carrie, John Carter, Helen Carrol
    C. Helen Carrol, James Carson, John Carter, Mary Carrie
    D. John Carter, Helen Carrol, Mary Carrie, James Carson

1.____

2. The one of the following which lists the names of persons in the CORRECT alphabetical order is:

    A. Jones, John C.; Jones, John A.; Jones, John P.; Jones, John K.
    B. Jones, John P.; Jones, John K.; Jones, John C.; Jones, John A.
    C. Jones, John A.; Jones, John C.; Jones, John K.; Jones, John P.
    D. Jones, John K.; Jones, John C.; Jones, John A.; Jones, John P.

2.____

3. The one of the following which lists the names of the companies in the CORRECT alphabetical order is:

    A. Blane Co., Blake Co., Block Co., Blear Co.
    B. Blake Co., Blane Co., Blear Co., Block Co.
    C. Block Co., Blear Co., Blane Co., Blake Co.
    D. Blear Co., Blake Co., Blane Co., Block Co.

3.____

4. You are to return to the file an index card on *Barry C. Wayne Materials and Supplies Co.* Of the following, the CORRECT alphabetical group that you should return the index card to is

    A. A to G   B. H to M   C. N to S   D. T to Z

4.____

Questions 5-10.

DIRECTIONS: In each of Questions 5 through 10, the names of four people are given. For each question, choose as your answer the one of the four names given which should be filed FIRST according to the usual system of alphabetical filing of names, as described in the following paragraph.

In filing names, you must start with the last name. Names are filed in order of the first letter of the last name, then the second letter, etc. Therefore, BAILY would be filed before BROWN, which would be filed before COLT. A name with fewer letters of the same type comes first; i.e., Smith before Smithe. If the last names are the same, the names are filed alphabetically by the first name. If the first name is an initial, a name with an initial would come before a first name that starts with the same letter as the initial. Therefore, I. BROWN would come before IRA BROWN. Finally, if both last name and first name are the same, the name would be filed alphabetically by the middle name, once again an initial coming before a middle name which starts with the same letter as the initial. If there is no middle name at all, the name would come before those with middle initials or names.

> Sample Question: A. Lester Daniels
> B. William Dancer
> C. Nathan Danzig
> D. Dan Lester

The last names beginning with D are filed before the last name beginning with L. Since DANIELS, DANCER, and DANZIG all begin with the same three letters, you must look at the fourth letter of the last name to determine which name should be filed first. C comes before I or Z in the alphabet, so DANCER is filed before DANIELS or DANZIG. Therefore, the answer to the above sample question is B.

5.   A. Scott Biala   5._____
      B. Mary Byala
      C. Martin Baylor
      D. Francis Bauer

6.   A. Howard J. Black   6._____
      B. Howard Black
      C. J. Howard Black
      D. John H. Black

7.   A. Theodora Garth Kingston   7._____
      B. Theadore Barth Kingston
      C. Thomas Kingston
      D. Thomas T. Kingston

8.   A. Paulette Mary Huerta   8._____
      B. Paul M. Huerta
      C. Paulette L. Huerta
      D. Peter A. Huerta

9.   A. Martha Hunt Morgan   9._____
      B. Martin Hunt Morgan
      C. Mary H. Morgan
      D. Martine H. Morgan

10.   A. James T. Meerschaum   10._____
      B. James M. Mershum
      C. James F. Mearshaum
      D. James N. Meshum

Questions 11-14.

DIRECTIONS: Questions 11 through 14 are to be answered SOLELY on the basis of the following information.

You are required to file various documents in file drawers which are labeled according to the following pattern:

DOCUMENTS

MEMOS		LETTERS	
File	Subject	File	Subject
84PM1 - (A-L)		84PC1 - (A-L)	
84PM2 - (M-Z)		84PC2 - (M-Z)	

REPORTS		INQUIRIES	
File	Subject	File	Subject
84PR1 - (A-L)		84PQ1 - (A-L)	
84PR2 - (M-Z)		84PQ2 - (M-Z)	

11.   A letter dealing with a burglary should be filed in the drawer labeled   11._____

     A. 84PM1   B. 84PC1   C. 84PR1   D. 84PQ2

12.   A report on Statistics should be found in the drawer labeled   12._____

     A. 84PM1   B. 84PC2   C. 84PR2   D. 84PQ2

13.   An inquiry is received about parade permit procedures. It should be filed in the drawer   13._____
labeled

     A. 84PM2   B. 84PC1   C. 84PR1   D. 84PQ2

14.   A police officer has a question about a robbery report you filed.   14._____
You should pull this file from the drawer labeled

     A. 84PM1   B. 84PM2   C. 84PR1   D. 84PR2

Questions 15-22.

DIRECTIONS: Each of Questions 15 through 22 consists of four or six numbered names. For each question, choose the option (A, B, C, or D) which indicates the order in which the names should be filed in accordance with the following filing instructions:
- File alphabetically according to last name, then first name, then middle initial.
- File according to each successive letter within a name.

- When comparing two names in which, the letters in the longer name are identical to the corresponding letters in the shorter name, the shorter name is filed first.
- When the last names are the same, initials are always filed before names beginning with the same letter.

15.   I.   Ralph Robinson
            II.   Alfred Ross
           III. Luis Robles
           IV. James Roberts

The CORRECT filing sequence for the above names should be

  A. IV, II, I, III   B. I, IV, III, II
  C. III, IV, I, II   D. IV, I, III, II

16.   I.   Irwin Goodwin
            II.   Inez Gonzalez
           III. Irene Goodman
           IV. Ira S. Goodwin
            V.   Ruth I. Goldstein
          VI. M.B. Goodman

The CORRECT filing sequence for the above names should be

  A. V, II, I, IV, III, VI   B. V, II, VI, III, IV, I
  C. V, II, III, VI, IV, I   D. V, II, III, VI, I, IV

17.   I.   George Allan
            II.   Gregory Allen
           III. Gary Allen
           IV. George Allen

The CORRECT filing sequence for the above names should be

  A. IV, III, I, II   B. I, IV, II, III
  C. III, IV, I, II   D. I, III, IV, II

18.   I.   Simon Kauffman
            II.   Leo Kaufman
           III. Robert Kaufmann
           IV. Paul Kauffmann

The CORRECT filing sequence for the above names should be

  A. I, IV, II, III   B. II, IV, III, I
  C. III, II, IV, I   D. I, II, III, IV

19.   I.   Roberta Williams
            II.   Robin Wilson
           III. Roberta Wilson
           IV. Robin Williams

The CORRECT filing sequence for the above names should be

  A. III, II, IV, I   B. I, IV, III, II
  C. I, II, III, IV   D. III, I, II, IV

15.___

16.___

17.___

18.___

19.___

20.
    I.   Lawrence Shultz
    II. Albert Schultz
    III. Theodore Schwartz
    IV. Thomas Schwarz
    V. Alvin Schultz
    VI. Leonard Shultz

The CORRECT filing sequence for the above names should be

  A. II, V, III, IV, I, VI   B. IV, III, V, I, II, VI
  C. II, V, I, VI, III, IV   D. I, VI, II, V, III, IV

20.____

21.
    I.   McArdle
    II. Mayer
    III. Maletz
    IV. McNiff
    V. Meyer
    VI. MacMahon

The CORRECT filing sequence for the above names should be

  A. I, IV, VI, III, II, V   B. II, I, IV, VI, III, V
  C. VI, III, II, I, IV, V   D. VI, III, II, V, I, IV

21.____

22.
    I.   Jack E. Johnson
    II. R.H. Jackson
    III. Bertha Jackson
    IV. J.T. Johnson
    V. Ann Johns
    VI. John Jacobs

The CORRECT filing sequence for the above names should be

  A. II, III, VI, V, IV, I   B. III, II, VI, V, IV, I
  C. VI, II, III, I, V, IV   D. III, II, VI, IV, V, I

22.____

Questions 23-30.

DIRECTIONS: The code table below shows 10 letters with matching numbers. For each question, there are three sets of letters. Each set of letters is followed by a set of numbers which may or may not match their correct letter according to the code table. For each question, check all three sets of letters and numbers and mark your answer:
    A. if no pairs are correctly matched
    B. if only one pair is correctly matched
    C. if only two pairs are correctly matched
    D. if all three pairs are correctly matched

CODE TABLE

T	M	V	D	S	P	R	G	B	H
1	2	3	4	5	6	7	8	9	0

Sample Question: TMVDSP - 123456
                 RGBHTM - 789011
                 DSPRGB - 256789

In the sample question above, the first set of numbers correctly matches its set of letters. But the second and third pairs contain mistakes. In the second pair, M is incorrectly matched with number 1. According to the code table, letter M should be correctly matched with number 2. In the third pair, the letter D is incorrectly matched with number 2. According to the code table, letter D should be correctly matched with number 4. Since only one of the pairs is correctly matched, the answer to this sample question is B.

23. RSBMRM 759262   23.____
  GDSRVH 845730
  VDBRTM 349713

24. TGVSDR 183247   24.____
  SMHRDP 520647
  TRMHSR 172057

25. DSPRGM 456782   25.____
  MVDBHT 234902
  HPMDBT 062491

26. BVPTRD 936184   26.____
  GDPHMB 807029
  GMRHMV 827032

27. MGVRSH 283750   27.____
  TRDMBS 174295
  SPRMGV 567283

28. SGBSDM 489542   28.____
  MGHPTM 290612
  MPBMHT 269301

29. TDPBHM 146902   29.____
  VPBMRS 369275
  GDMBHM 842902

30. MVPTBV 236194   30.____
  PDRTMB 647128
  BGTMSM 981232

KEY (CORRECT ANSWERS)

1.	A	11.	B	21.	C
2.	C	12.	C	22.	B
3.	B	13.	D	23.	B
4.	D	14.	D	24.	B
5.	D	15.	D	25.	C
6.	B	16.	C	26.	A
7.	B	17.	D	27.	D
8.	B	18.	A	28.	A
9.	A	19.	B	29.	D
10.	C	20.	A	30.	A

TEST 2

DIRECTIONS: Each question or incomplete statement is followed by several suggested answers or completions. Select the one that BEST answers the question or completes the statement. *PRINT THE LETTER OF THE CORRECT ANSWER IN THE SPACE AT THE RIGHT.*

Questions 1-10.

DIRECTIONS: Questions 1 through 10 each consists of two columns, each containing four lines of names, numbers and/or addresses. For each question, compare the lines in Column I with the lines in Column II to see if they match exactly, and mark your answer A, B, C, or D, according to the following instructions:
  A. all four lines match exactly
  B. only three lines match exactly
  C. only two lines match exactly
  D. only one line matches exactly

	COLUMN I	COLUMN II	
1.	I. Earl Hodgson II. 1409870 III. Shore Ave. IV. Macon Rd.	Earl Hodgson 1408970 Schore Ave. Macon Rd.	1.___
2.	I. 9671485 II. 470 Astor Court III. Halprin, Phillip IV. Frank D. Poliseo	9671485 470 Astor Court Halperin, Phillip Frank D. Poliseo	2.___
3.	I. Tandem Associates II. 144-17 Northern Blvd. III. Alberta Forchi IV. Kings Park, NY 10751	Tandom Associates 144-17 Northern Blvd. Albert Forchi Kings Point, NY 10751	3.___
4.	I. Bertha C. McCormack II. Clayton, MO. III. 976-4242 IV. New City, NY 10951	Bertha C. McCormack Clayton, MO. 976-4242 New City, NY 10951	4.___
5.	I. George C. Morill II. Columbia, SC 29201 III. Louis Ingham IV. 3406 Forest Ave.	George C. Morrill Columbia, SD 29201 Louis Ingham 3406 Forest Ave.	5.___
6.	I. 506 S. Elliott Pl. II. Herbert Hall III. 4712 Rockaway Pkway IV. 169 E. 7 St.	506 S. Elliott Pl. Hurbert Hall 4712 Rockaway Pkway 169 E. 7 St.	6.___

	COLUMN I	COLUMN II	

7.
I.	345 Park Ave.	345 Park Pl.
II.	Colman Oven Corp.	Coleman Oven Corp.
III.	Robert Conte	Robert Conti
IV.	6179846	6179846

7._____

8.
I.	Grigori Schierber	Grigori Schierber
II.	Des Moines, Iowa	Des Moines, Iowa
III.	Gouverneur Hospital	Gouverneur Hospital
IV.	91-35 Cresskill Pl.	91-35 Cresskill Pl.

8._____

9.
I.	Jeffery Janssen	Jeffrey Janssen
II.	8041071	8041071
III.	40 Rockefeller Plaza	40 Rockafeller Plaza
IV.	407 6 St.	406 7 St.

9._____

10.
I.	5971996	5871996
II.	3113 Knickerbocker Ave.	3113 Knickerbocker Ave.
III.	8434 Boston Post Rd.	8424 Boston Post Rd.
IV.	Penn Station	Penn Station

10._____

Questions 11-14.

DIRECTIONS: Questions 11 through 14 are to be answered by looking at the four groups of names and addresses listed below (I, II, III, and IV) and then finding out the number of groups that have their corresponding numbered lines exactly the same.

GROUP I
Line 1. Richmond General Hospital
Line 2. Geriatric Clinic
Line 3. 3975 Paerdegat St.
Line 4 Loudonville, New York 11538

GROUP II
Richman General Hospital
Geriatric Clinic
3975 Peardegat St.
Londonville, New York 11538

GROUP III
Line 1. Richmond General Hospital
Line 2. Geriatric Clinic
Line 3. 3795 Paerdegat St.
Line 4 Loudonville, New York 11358

GROUP IV
Richmend General Hospital
Geriatric Clinic
3975 Paerdegat St.
Loudonville, New York 11538

11. In how many groups is line one exactly the same?

11._____

   A. Two   B. Three   C. Four   D. None

12. In how many groups is line two exactly the same?

12._____

   A. Two   B. Three   C. Four   D. None

13. In how many groups is line three exactly the same?

13._____

   A. Two   B. Three   C. Four   D. None

14. In how many groups is line four exactly the same?　14.___

 A. Two B. Three C. Four D. None

Questions 15-18.

DIRECTIONS: Each of Questions 15 through 18 has two lists of names and addresses. Each list contains three sets of names and addresses. Check each of the three sets in the list on the right to see if they are the same as the corresponding set in the list on the left. Mark your answers:
 A. if none of the sets in the right list are the same as those in the left list
 B. if only one of the sets in the right list is the same as those in the left list
 C. if only two of the sets in the right list are the same as those in the left list
 D. if all three sets in the right list are the same as those in the left list

15. Mary T. Berlinger   Mary T. Berlinger   15.___
  2351 Hampton St.   2351 Hampton St.
  Monsey, N.Y. 20117   Monsey, N.Y. 20117

  Eduardo Benes   Eduardo Benes
  473 Kingston Avenue   473 Kingston Avenue
  Central Islip, N.Y. 11734   Central Islip, N.Y. 11734

  Alan Carrington Fuchs   Alan Carrington Fuchs
  17 Gnarled Hollow Road   17 Gnarled Hollow Road
  Los Angeles, CA 91635   Los Angeles, CA 91685

16. David John Jacobson   David John Jacobson   16.___
  178 35 St. Apt. 4C   178 53 St. Apt. 4C
  New York, N.Y. 00927   New York, N.Y. 00927

  Ann-Marie Calonella   Ann-Marie Calonella
  7243 South Ridge Blvd.   7243 South Ridge Blvd.
  Bakersfield, CA 96714   Bakersfield, CA 96714

  Pauline M. Thompson   Pauline M. Thomson
  872 Linden Ave.   872 Linden Ave.
  Houston, Texas 70321   Houston, Texas 70321

17. Chester LeRoy Masterton Chester LeRoy Masterson 17.___
  152 Lacy Rd.   152 Lacy Rd.
  Kankakee, Ill. 54532   Kankakee, Ill. 54532

  William Maloney   William Maloney
  S. LaCrosse Pla.   S. LaCross Pla.
  Wausau, Wisconsin 52146   Wausau, Wisconsin 52146

  Cynthia V. Barnes   Cynthia V. Barnes
  16 Pines Rd.   16 Pines Rd.
  Greenpoint, Miss. 20376   Greenpoint, Miss. 20376

18.　Marcel Jean Frontenac
　　　8 Burton On The Water
　　　Calender, Me. 01471

　　　J. Scott Marsden
　　　174 S. Tipton St.
　　　Cleveland, Ohio

　　　Lawrence T. Haney
　　　171 McDonough St.
　　　Decatur, Ga. 31304

　　　Marcel Jean Frontenac
　　　6 Burton On The Water
　　　Calender, Me. 01471

　　　J. Scott Marsden
　　　174 Tipton St.
　　　Cleveland, Ohio

　　　Lawrence T. Haney
　　　171 McDonough St.
　　　Decatur, Ga. 31304

18.____

Questions 19-26.

DIRECTIONS:　Each of Questions 19 through 26 has two lists of numbers. Each list contains three sets of numbers. Check each of the three sets in the list on the right to see if they are the same as the corresponding set in the list on the left. Mark your answers:
A.　if none of the sets in the right list are the same as those in the left list
B.　if only one of the sets in the right list is the same as those in the left list
C.　if only two of the sets in the right list are the same as those in the left list
D.　if all three sets in the right list are the same as those in the left list

19.　7354183476
　　　4474747744
　　　57914302311

　　　7354983476
　　　4474747774
　　　57914302311

19.____

20.　7143592185
　　　8344517699
　　　9178531263

　　　7143892185
　　　8344518699
　　　9178531263

20.____

21.　2572114731
　　　8806835476
　　　8255831246

　　　257214731
　　　8806835476
　　　8255831246

21.____

22.　331476853821
　　　6976658532996
　　　3766042113715

　　　331476858621
　　　6976655832996
　　　3766042113745

22.____

23.　8806663315
　　　74477138449
　　　211756663666

　　　8806663315
　　　74477138449
　　　211756663666

23.____

24.　990006966996
　　　53022219743
　　　4171171117717

　　　99000696996
　　　53022219843
　　　4171171177717

24.____

25.　24400222433004
　　　5300030055000355
　　　20000075532002022

　　　24400222433004
　　　5300030055500355
　　　20000075532002022

25.____

26.   611166640660001116   61116664066001116   26.____
       7111300117001100733   7111300117001100733
       26666446664476518   26666446664476518

Questions 27-30.

DIRECTIONS: Questions 27 through 30 are to be answered by picking the answer which is in the correct numerical order, from the lowest number to the highest number, in each question.

27.   A.   44533, 44518, 44516, 44547   27.____
        B.   44516, 44518, 44533, 44547
        C.   44547, 44533, 44518, 44516
        D.   44518, 44516, 44547, 44533

28.   A.   95587, 95593, 95601, 95620   28.____
        B.   95601, 95620, 95587, 95593
        C.   95593, 95587, 95601, 95620
        D.   95620, 95601, 95593, 95587

29.   A.   232212, 232208, 232232, 232223   29.____
        B.   232208, 232223, 232212, 232232
        C.   232208, 232212, 232223, 232232
        D.   232223, 232232, 232208, 232212

30.   A.   113419, 113521, 113462, 113588   30.____
        B.   113588, 113462, 113521, 113419
        C.   113521, 113588, 113419, 113462
        D.   113419, 113462, 113521, 113588

KEY (CORRECT ANSWERS)

1.	C	11.	A	21.	C
2.	B	12.	C	22.	A
3.	D	13.	A	23.	D
4.	A	14.	A	24.	A
5.	C	15.	C	25.	C
6.	B	16.	B	26.	C
7.	D	17.	B	27.	B
8.	A	18.	B	28.	A
9.	D	19.	B	29.	C
10.	C	20.	B	30.	D

CODING

COMMENTARY

An ingenious question-type called coding, involving elements of alphabetizing, filing, name and number comparison, and evaluative judgment and application, has currently won wide acceptance in testing circles for measuring clerical aptitude and general ability, particularly on the senior (middle) grades (levels).

While the directions for this question usually vary in detail, the candidate is generally asked to consider groups of names, codes, and numbers, and, then, according to a given plan, to arrange codes in alphabetic order; to arrange these in numerical sequence; to re-arrange columns of names and numbers in correct order; to espy errors in coding; to choose the correct coding arrangement in consonance with the given directions and examples, etc.

This question-type appears to have few paramaters in respect to form, substance, or degree of difficulty.

Accordingly, acquaintance with, and practice in, the coding question is recommended for the serious candidate.

EXAMINATION SECTION
TEST 1

DIRECTIONS:

CODE TABLE

Name of Applicant	H	A	N	G	S	B	R	U	K	E
Test Code	c	o	m	p	l	e	x	i	t	y
File Number	0	1	2	3	4	5	6	7	8	9

Assume that each of the above *capital letters* is the first letter of the Name of an Applicant, that the *small letter* directly beneath each capital letter is the Test Code for the Applicant, and that the *number* directly beneath each code letter is the File Number for the Applicant.
In each of the following questions, the test code letters and the file numbers in Columns 2 and 3 should correspond to the capital letters in Column 1. For each question, look at each column carefully and mark your answer as follows:

If there is an error only in Column 2, mark your answer A.
If there is an error only in Column 3, mark your answer B.
If there is an error in both Columns 2 and 3, mark your answer C.
If both Columns 2 and 3 are correct, mark your answer D.

The following sample question is given to help you understand the procedure.

SAMPLE QUESTION

Column 1	Column 2	Column 3
AKEHN	otyci	18902

In Column 2, the final test code letter "i" should be "m." Column 3 is correctly coded to Column 1. Since there is an error only in Column 2, the answer is A

	Column 1	Column 2	Column 3	
1.	NEKKU	mytti	29987	1.__
2.	KRAEB	txlye	86095	2.__
3.	ENAUK	ymoit	92178	3.__
4.	REANA	xeomo	69121	4.__
5.	EKHSE	ytcxy	97049	5.__

KEY (CORRECT ANSWERS)

1. B
2. C
3. D
4. A
5. C

TEST 2

DIRECTIONS: The employee identification codes in Column I begin and end with a capital letter and have an eight-digit number in between. In Questions 1 through 8,
employee identification codes in Column I are to be arranged according to the
following rules:

First: Arrange in alphabetical order according to the first letter.

Second: When two or more employee identification codes have the same first letter,
arrange in alphabetical order according to the last letter.

Third: When two or more employee codes have the same first and last letters,
arrange in numerical order beginning with the lowest number.

The employee identification codes in Column I are numbered 1 through 5 in the order in which
they are listed. In Column II the numbers 1 through 5 are arranged in four different ways to show
different arrangements of the corresponding employee identification numbers. Choose the
answer in Column II in which the employee identification numbers are arranged according to the
above rules.

SAMPLE QUESTION

Column I	Column II
1. E75044127B	A. 4, 1, 3, 2, 5
2. B96399104A	B. 4, 1, 2, 3, 5
3. B93939086A	C. 4, 3, 2, 5, 1
4. B47064465H	D. 3, 2, 5, 4, 1
5. B99040922A	

In the sample question, the four employee identification codes starting with B should be put
before the employee identification code starting with E. The employee identification codes starting with B and ending with A should be put before the employee identification codes starting
with B and ending with H. The three employee identification codes starting with B and ending
with A should be listed in numerical order, beginning with the lowest number. The correct way to
arrange the employee identification codes, therefore, is 3, 2, 5, 4, 1 shown below.

    3.   B93939086A
    2.   B96399104A
    5.   B99040922A
    4.   B47064465H
    1.   E75044127B

Therefore, the answer to the sample question is D. Now answer the following questions according to the above rules.

Column I	Column II	
1. 1. G42786441J	A. 2, 5, 4, 3, 1	1.____
2. H45665413J	B. 5, 4, 1, 3, 2	
3. G43117690J	C. 4, 5, 1, 3, 2	
4. G43546698I	D. 1, 3, 5, 4, 2	
5. G41679942I		

2.	1.	S44556178T	A.	1, 3, 5, 2, 4	2.___
	2.	T43457169T	B.	4, 3, 5, 2, 1	
	3.	S53321176T	C.	5, 3, 1, 2, 4	
	4.	T53317998S	D.	5, 1, 3, 4, 2	
	5.	S67673942S			
3.	1.	R63394217D	A.	5, 4, 2, 3, 1	3.___
	2.	R63931247D	B.	1, 5, 3, 2, 4	
	3.	R53931247D	C.	5, 3, 1, 2, 4	
	4.	R66874239D	D.	5, 1, 2, 3, 4	
	4.	R46799366D			
4.	1.	A35671968B	A.	3, 2, 1, 4, 5	4.___
	2.	A35421794C	B.	2, 3, 1, 5, 4	
	3.	A35466987B	C.	1, 3, 2, 4, 5	
	4.	C10435779A	D.	3, 1, 2, 4, 5	
	5.	C00634779B			
5.	1.	I99746426Q	A.	2, 1, 3, 5, 4	5.___
	2.	I10445311Q	B.	5, 4, 2, 1, 3	
	3.	J63749877P	C.	4, 5, 3, 2, 1	
	4.	J03421739Q	D.	2, 1, 4, 5, 3	
	5.	J00765311Q			
6.	1.	M33964217N	A.	4, 1, 5, 2, 3	6.___
	2.	N33942770N	B.	5, 1, 4, 3, 2	
	3.	N06155881M	C.	4, 1, 5, 3, 2	
	4.	M00433669M	D.	1, 4, 5, 2, 3	
	5.	M79034577N			
7.	1.	D77643905C	A.	1, 2, 5, 3, 4	7.___
	2.	D44106788C	B.	5, 3, 2, 1, 4	
	3.	D13976022F	C.	2, 1, 5, 3, 4	
	4.	D97655430E	D.	2, 1, 4, 5, 3	
	5.	D00439776F			
8.	1.	W22746920A	A.	2, 1, 3, 4, 5	8.___
	2.	W22743720A	B.	2, 1, 5, 3, 4	
	3.	W32987655A	C.	1, 2, 3, 4, 5	
	4.	W43298765A	D.	1, 2, 5, 3, 4	
	5.	W30987433A			

KEY (CORRECT ANSWERS)

1.	B		5.	A
2.	D		6.	C
3.	C		7.	D
4.	D		8.	B

TEST 3

DIRECTIONS: Each of the following equestions consists of three sets of names and name codes. In each question, the two names and name codes on the same line are supposed to be exactly the same.

Look carefully at each set of names and codes and mark your answer:
- A. if there are mistakes in all three sets
- B. if there are mistakes in two of the sets
- C. if there is a mistake in only one set
- D. if there are no mistakes in any of the sets

The following sample question is given to help you understand the procedure.

Macabe, John N. - V 53162	Macade, John N. - V 53162
Howard, Joan S. - J 24791	Howard, Joan S. - J 24791
Ware, Susan B. - A 45068	Ware, Susan B. - A 45968

In the above sample question, the names and name codes of the first set are not exactly the same because of the spelling of the last name (Macabe - Macade). The names and name codes of the second set are exactly the same. The names and name codes of the third set are not exactly the same because the two name codes are different (A 45068 - A 45968), Since there are mistakes in only 2 of the sets, the answer to the sample question is B.

1. Powell, Michael C. - 78537 F
   Martinez, Pablo, J. - 24435 P
   MacBane, Eliot M. - 98674 E

   Powell, Michael C. - 78537 F
   Martinez, Pablo J. - 24435 P
   MacBane, Eliot M. - 98674 E

   1.____

2. Fitz-Kramer Machines Inc. - 259090
   Marvel Cleaning Service - 482657
   Donate, Carl G. - 637418

   Fitz-Kramer Machines Inc. - 259090
   Marvel Cleaning Service - 482657
   Danato, Carl G. - 687418

   2.____

3. Martin Davison Trading Corp. - 43108 T
   Cotwald Lighting Fixtures - 76065 L
   R. Crawford Plumbers - 23157 C

   Martin Davidson Trading Corp. - 43108 T
   Cotwald Lighting Fixtures - 70056 L
   R. Crawford Plumbers - 23157 G

   3.____

4. Fraiman Engineering Corp. - M4773
   Neuman, Walter B. - N7745
   Pierce, Eric M. - W6304

   Friaman Engineering Corp. -M4773
   Neumen, Walter B. - N7745
   Pierce, Eric M. - W6304

   4.____

5. Constable, Eugene - B 64837
   Derrick, Paul - H 27119
   Heller, Karen - S 49606

   Comstable, Eugene - B 64837
   Derrik, Paul - H 27119
   Heller, Karen - S 46906

   5.____

6. Hernando Delivery Service Co. - D 7456
   Barettz Electrical Supplies - N 5392
   Tanner, Abraham - M 4798

   Hernando Delivery Service Co. - D 7456
   Barettz Electrical Supplies - N 5392
   Tanner, Abraham - M 4798

   6.____

7. Kalin Associates - R 38641
   Sealey, Robert E. - P 63533
   Scalsi Office Furniture

   Kaline Associates - R 38641
   Sealey, Robert E. - P 63553
   Scalsi Office Furniture

   7.____

8. Janowsky, Philip M.- 742213
    Hansen, Thomas H. - 934816
    L. Lester and Son Inc. - 294568

Janowsky, Philip M.- 742213
Hanson, Thomas H. - 934816
L. Lester and Son Inc. - 294568

8.___

———

KEY (CORRECT ANSWERS)

1. D
2. C
3. A
4. B
5. A

6. D
7. B
8. C

———

TEST 4

DIRECTIONS: The following questions are to be answered on the basis of the following Code Table. In this table, for each number, a corresponding code letter is given. Each of the questions contains three pairs of numbers and code letters. In each pair, the code letters should correspond with the numbers in accordance with the Code Table.

	CODE TABLE									
Number	1	2	3	4	5	6	7	8	9	0
Corresponding Code Letter	Y	N	Z	X	W	T	U	P	S	R

In some of the pairs below, an error exists in the coding. Examine the pairs in each question carefully. If an error exists in:

Only one of the pairs in the question, mark your answer A.
Any two pairs in the question, mark your answer B.
All three pairs in the question, mark your answer C.
None of the pairs in the question, mark your answer D.

SAMPLE QUESTION

37258   -   ZUNWP
948764   -   SXPTTX
73196   -   UZYSP

In the above sample, the first pair is correct since each number, as listed, has the correct corresponding code letter. In the second pair, an error exists because the number 7 should have the code letter U instead of the letter T. In the third pair, an error exists because the number 6 should have the code letter T instead of the letter P. Since there are errors in two of the three pairs, the correct answer is B.

1. 493785   -   XSZUPW   1.____
   86398207 -   PTUSPNRU
   5943162   -   WSXZYTN

2. 5413968412 -   WXYZSTPXYR   2.____
   8763451297 -   PUTZXWYZSU
   4781965302 -   XUPYSUWZRN

3. 79137584 -   USYRUWPX   3.____
   638247   -   TZPNXS
   49679312 -   XSTUSZYN

4. 37854296 -   ZUPWXNST   4.____
   09183298 -   RSYXZNSP
   91762358 -   SYUTNXWP

5. 3918762485 -   ZSYPUTNXPW   5.____
   1578291436 -   YWUPNSYXZT
   2791385674 -   NUSYZPWTUX

6. 197546821 - YSUWSTPNY   6.____
    873024867 - PUZRNWPTU
    583179246 - WPZYURNXT

7. 510782463 - WYRUSNXTZ   7.____
    478192356 - XUPYSNZWT
    961728532 - STYUNPWXN

————

KEY (CORRECT ANSWERS)

1. A
2. C
3. B
4. B
5. D

6. C
7. B

————

TEST 5

DIRECTIONS: Assume that each of the capital letters is the first letter of the name of a city using EAM equipment. The number directly beneath each capital letter is the code number for the city. The small letter beneath each code number is the code letter for the number of EAM divisions in the city and the + or - symbol directly beneath each code letter is the code symbol which signifies whether or not the city uses third generation computers with the EAM equipment.

The questions that follow show City Letters in Column I, Code Numbers in Column II, Code Letters in Column III, and Code Symbols in Column IV. If correct. each City Letter in Column I should correspond by position with each of the three codes shown in the other three columns, in accordance with the coding key shown. *BUT* there are some errors. For each question,

> If there is a total of *ONE* error in Columns 2, 3, and 4, mark your answer A.
> If there is a total of *TWO* errors in Columns 2, 3, and 4, mark your answer B.
> If there is a total of *THREE* errors in Columns 2, 3, and 4, mark your answer C.
> If Columns 2, 3, and 4 are correct, mark your answer D.

SAMPLE QUESTION

I	II	III	IV
City Letter	Code Numbers	Code Letters	Code Symbols
Y J M O S	5 3 7 9 8	e b g i h	- - + + -

The errors are as follows: In Column 2, the Code Number should be "2" instead of "3" for City Letter "J," and in Column 4 the Code Symbol should be "+" instead of "-" for City Letter "Y." Since there is a total of two errors in Columns 2, 3, and 4, the answer to this sample question is B.

Now answer questions 1 through 9 according to these rules.

CODING KEY

City Letter	P	J	R	T	Y	K	M	S	0
Code Number	1	2	3	4	5	6	7	8	9
Code Letter	a	b	c	d	e	f	g	h	i
Code Symbol	+	-	+	-	+	-	+	-	+

	I	II	III	IV	
	City Letters	Code Numbers	Code Letters	Code Symbols	
1.	K O R M P	6 9 3 7 1	f i e g a	- - + + +	1.____
2.	O T P S Y	9 4 1 8 6	b d a h e	+ - - - +	2.____
3.	R S J T M	3 8 1 4 7	c h b e g	- - - - +	3.____
4.	P M S K J	1 7 8 6 2	a g h f b	+ + - - -	4.____
5.	M Y T J R	7 5 4 2 3	g e d f c	+ + - - +	5.____
6.	T P K Y O	4 1 6 7 9	d a f e i	- + - + -	6.____
7.	S K O R T	8 6 9 3 5	h f i c d	- - + + -	7.____
8.	J R Y P K	2 3 5 1 9	b d e a f	- + + + -	8.____
9.	R O M P Y	4 9 7 1 5	c i g a d	+ + - + +	9.____

KEY (CORRECT ANSWERS)

1. B
2. C
3. C
4. D
5. A

6. B
7. A
8. B
9. C

_____

TEST 6

Assume that each of the capital letters is the first letter of the name of an offense, that the small letter directly beneath each capital letter is the code letter for the offense, and that the number directly beneath each code letter is the file number for the offense.

DIRECTIONS: In each of the following questions, the code letters and file numbers should correspond to the capital letters.

If there is an error only in Column 2, mark your answer A.
If there is an error only in Column 3, mark your answer B.
If there is an error in both Column 2 and Column 3, mark your answer C.
If both Columns 2 and 3 are correct, mark your answer D.

SAMPLE QUESTION

Column 1	Column 2	Column 3
BNARGHSVVU	emoxtylcci	6357905118

The code letters in Column 2 are correct but the first "5" in Column 3 should be "2." Therefore, the answer is B. Now answer the following questions according to the above rules.

CODE TABLE

Name of Offense	V	A	N	D	S	B	R	U	G	H
Code Letter	c	o	m	p	l	e	x	i	t	y
File Number	1	2	3	4	5	6	7	8	9	0

	Column 1	Column 2	Column 3	
1.	HGDSBNBSVR	ytplxmelcx	0945736517	1.____
2.	SDGUUNHVAH	lptiimycoy	5498830120	2.____
3.	BRSNAAVUDU	exlmooctpi	6753221848	3.____
4.	VSRUDNADUS	cleipmopil	1568432485	4.____
5.	NDSHVRBUAG	mplycxeiot	3450175829	5.____
6.	GHUSNVBRDA	tyilmcexpo	9085316742	6.____
7.	DBSHVURANG	pesycixomt	4650187239	7.____
8.	RHNNASBDGU	xymnolepti	7033256398	8.____

KEY (CORRECT ANSWERS)

1. C
2. D
3. A
4. C
5. B

6. D
7. A
8. C

TEST 7

DIRECTIONS: Each of the following questions contains three sets of code letters and code numbers. In each set, the code numbers should correspond with the code letters as given in the Table, but there is a coding error in some of the sets. Examine the sets in each question carefully.

Mark your answer A if there is a coding error in only *ONE* of the sets in the question.
Mark your answer B if there is a coding error in any *TWO* of the sets in the question.
Mark your answer C if there is a coding error in all *THREE* sets in the question.
Mark your answer D if there is a coding error in *NONE* of the sets in the question.

SAMPLE QUESTION

fgzduwaf   -   35720843
uabsdgfw   -   04262538
hhfaudgs   -   99340257

In the above sample question, the first set is right because each code number matches the code letter as in the Code Table. In the second set, the corresponding number for the code letter b is wrong because it should be 1 instead of 2. In the third set, the corresponding number for the last code letter s is wrong because it should be 6 instead of 7. Since there is an error in two of the sets, the answer to the above sample question is B.

In the Code Table below, each code letter has a corresponding code number directly beneath it.

CODE TABLE

Code Letter	b	d	f	a	g	s	z	w	h	u
Code Number	1	2	3	4	5	6	7	8	9	0

1. fsbughwz - 36104987   zwubgasz - 78025467   1._____
    ghgufddb - 59583221

2. hafgdaas - 94351446   ddsfabsd - 22734162   2._____
    wgdbssgf - 85216553

3. abfbssbd - 41316712   ghzfaubs - 59734017   3._____
    sdbzfwza - 62173874

4. whfbdzag - 89412745   daaszuub - 24467001   4._____
    uzhfwssd - 07936623

5. zbadgbuh - 71425109   dzadbbsz - 27421167   5._____
    gazhwaff - 54798433

6. fbfuadsh - 31304265   gzfuwzsb - 57300671   6._____
    bashhgag - 14699535

KEY (CORRECT ANSWERS)

1. B
2. C
3. B
4. B
5. D
6. C

————

TEST 8

DIRECTIONS: The following questions are to be answered on the basis of the following Code Table. In this table every letter has a corresponding code number to be punched. Each question contains three pairs of letters and code numbers. In each pair, the code numbers should correspond with the letters in accordance with the Code Table.

CODE TABLE

Letter	P	L	A	N	D	C	0	B	U	R
Corresponding Code Number	1	2	3	4	5	6	7	8	9	0

In some of the pairs below, an error exists in the coding. Examine the pairs in each question. Mark your answer

A if there is a mistake in only *one* of the pairs
B if there is a mistake in only *two* of the pairs
C if there is a mistake in *all three* of the pairs
D if there is a mistake in *none* of the pairs

SAMPLE QUESTION

LCBPUPAB - 26819138
ACOABOL   - 3683872
NDURONUC - 46901496

In the above sample, the first pair is correct since each letter as listed has the correct corresponding code number. In the second pair, an error exists because the letter 0 should have the code number 7, instead of 8. In the third pair, an error exists because the letter D should have the code number 5, instead of 6. Since there are errors in two of the three pairs, your answer should be B.

1. ADCANPLC - 35635126   DORURBBO - 57090877   1.____
   PNACBUCP - 14368061

2. LCOBLRAP - 26782931   UPANUPCD - 91349156   2.____
   RLDACLRO - 02536207

3. LCOROPAR - 26707130   BALANRUP - 83234091   3.____
   DOPOAULL - 57173922

4. ONCRUBAP - 74609831   DCLANORD - 56243705   4.____
   AORPDUR - 3771590

5. PANRBUCD - 13408965   UAOCDPLR - 93765120   5.____
   OPDDOBRA - 71556803

6. BAROLDCP - 83072561   PNOCOBLA - 14767823   6.____
   BURPDOLA - 89015723

7. ANNCPABO - 34461387   DBALDRCP - 58325061   7.____
   ACRPOUL - 3601792

8. BLAPOUR - 8321790   NOACNPL - 4736412   8._____
    RODACORD - 07536805

9. ADUBURCL- 3598062   NOCOBAPR - 47578310   9._____
    PRONDALU - 10754329

10. UBADCLOR - 98356270   NBUPPARA - 48911033   10._____
    LONDUPRC - 27459106

_____

KEY (CORRECT ANSWERS)

1. C
2. B
3. D
4. B
5. A

6. D
7. B
8. B
9. C
10. A

_____

TEST 9

DIRECTIONS: Answer questions 1 through 10 ONLY on the basis of the following information.
    Column I consists of serial numbers of dollar bills. Column II shows different ways of arranging the corresponding serial numbers.
    The serial numbers of dollar bills in Column I begin and end with a capital letter and have an eight-digit number in between. The serial numbers in Column I are to be arranged according to the following rules:

FIRST: In alphabetical order according to the first letter.

SECOND: When two or more serial numbers have the same first letter, in alphabetical order according to the last letter.

THIRD: When two or more serial numbers have the same first <u>and</u> last letters, in numerical order, beginning with the lowest number.

The serial numbers in Column I are numbered (1) through (5) in the order in which they are listed. In Column II the numbers (1) through (5) are arranged in four different ways to show different arrangements of the corresponding serial numbers. Choose the answer in Column II in which the serial numbers are arranged according to the above rules.

SAMPLE QUESTION

	COLUMN I		COLUMN II
(1)	E75044127B	(A)	4, 1, 3, 2, 5
(2)	B96399104A	(B)	4, 1, 2, 3, 5
(3)	B93939086A	(C)	4, 3, 2, 5, 1
(4)	B47064465H	(D)	3, 2, 5, 4, 1
(5)	B99040922A		

In the sample question, the four serial numbers starting with B should be put before the serial number starting with E. The serial numbers starting with B and ending with A should be put before the serial number starting with B and ending with H. The three serial numbers starting with B and ending with A should be listed in numerical order, beginning with the lowest number. The correct way to arrange the serial numbers, therefore, is:

(3)	B93939086A
(2)	B96399104A
(5)	B99040922A
(4)	B47064465H
(1)	E75044127B

Since the order of arrangement is 3, 2, 5, 4, 1, the answer to the sample question is (D).

		COLUMN I		COLUMN II				
1.	(1)	P44343314Y	A.	2,	3,	1,	4,	5
	(2)	P44141341S	B.	1,	5,	3,	2,	4
	(3)	P44141431L	C.	4,	2,	3,	5,	1
	(4)	P41143413W	D.	5,	3,	2,	4,	1
	(5)	P44313433H						
2.	(1)	D89077275M	A.	3,	2,	5,	4,	1
	(2)	D98073724N	B.	1,	4,	3,	2,	5
	(3)	D90877274N	C.	4,	1,	5,	2,	3
	(4)	D98877275M	D.	1,	3,	2,	5,	4
	(5)	D98873725N						

3.	(1)	H32548137E		A.	2,	4,	5,	1,	3
	(2)	H35243178A		B.	1,	5,	2,	3,	4
	(3)	H35284378F		C.	1,	5,	2,	4,	3
	(4)	H35288337A		D.	2,	1,	5,	3,	4
	(5)	H32883173B							
4.	(1)	K24165039H		A.	4,	2,	5,	3,	1
	(2)	F24106599A		B.	2,	3,	4,	1,	5
	(3)	L21406639G		C.	4,	2,	5,	1,	3
	(4)	C24156093A		D.	1,	3,	4,	5,	2
	(5)	K24165593D							
5.	(1)	H79110642E		A.	2,	1,	3,	5,	4
	(2)	H79101928E		B.	2,	1,	4,	5,	3
	(3)	A79111567F		C.	3,	5,	2,	1,	4
	(4)	H79111796E		D.	4,	3,	5,	1,	2
	(5)	A79111618F							
6.	(1)	P16388385W		A.	3,	4,	5,	2,	1
	(2)	R16388335V		B.	2,	3,	4,	5,	1
	(3)	P16383835W		C.	2,	4,	3,	1,	5
	(4)	R18386865V		D.	3,	1,	5,	2,	4
	(5)	P18686865W							
7.	(1)	B42271749G		A.	4,	1,	5,	2,	3
	(2)	B42271779G		B.	4,	1,	2,	5,	3
	(3)	E43217779G		C.	1,	2,	4,	5,	3
	(4)	B42874119C		D.	5,	3,	1,	2,	4
	(5)	E42817749G							
8.	(1)	M57906455S		A.	4,	1,	5,	3,	2
	(2)	N87077758S		B.	3,	4,	1,	5,	2
	(3)	N87707757B		C.	4,	1,	5,	2,	3
	(4)	M57877759B		D.	1,	5,	3,	2,	4
	(5)	M57906555S							
9.	(1)	C69336894Y		A.	2,	5,	3,	1,	4
	(2)	C69336684V		B.	3,	2,	5,	1,	4
	(3)	C69366887W		C.	3,	1,	4,	5,	2
	(4)	C69366994Y		D.	2,	5,	1,	3,	4
	(5)	C69336865V							
10.	(1)	A56247181D		A.	1,	5,	3,	2,	4
	(2)	A56272128P		B.	3,	1,	5,	2,	4
	(3)	H56247128D		C.	3,	2,	1,	5,	4
	(4)	H56272288P		D.	1,	5,	2,	3,	4
	(5)	A56247188D							

_____

KEY (CORRECT ANSWERS)

1.	D	6.	D
2.	B	7.	B
3.	A	8.	A
4.	C	9.	A
5.	C	10.	D

_____

TEST 10

DIRECTIONS: Answer the following questions on the basis of the instructions, the code, and the sample questions given below. Assume that an officer at a certain location is equipped with a two-way radio to keep him in constant touch with his security headquarters. Radio messages and replies are given in code form, as follows:

CODE TABLE

Radio Code for Situation	J	P	M	F	B
Radio Code for Action to be Taken	o	r	a	z	q
Radio Response for Action Being Taken	1	2	3	4	5

Assume that each of the above capital letters is the radio code for a particular type of situation, that the small letter below each capital letter is the radio code for the action an officer is directed to take, and that the number directly below each small letter is the radio response an officer should make to indicate what action was actually taken.

In each of the following questions, the code letter for the action directed (Column 2) and the code number for the action taken (Column 3) should correspond to the capital letters in Column 1.

INSTRUCTIONS: If only Column 2 is different from Column 1, mark your answer I.
If only Column 3 is different from Column 1, mark your answer II.
If both Column 2 and Column 3 are different from Column I, mark your answer III.
If both Columns 2 and 3 are the same as Column 1, mark your answer IV.

SAMPLE QUESTION

Column 1	Column 2	Column 3
JPFMB	orzaq	12453

The CORRECT answer is: A. I B. II C. III D. IV
The code letters in Column 2 are correct, but the numbers "53" in Column 3 should be "35." Therefore, the answer is B. Now answe the following questions according to the above rules.

	Column 1	Column 2	Column 3	
1.	PBFJM	rqzoa	25413	1.____
2.	MPFBJ	zrqao	32541	2.____
3.	JBFPM	oqzra	15432	3.____
4.	BJPMF	qaroz	51234	4.____
5.	PJFMB	rozaq	21435	5.____
6.	FJBMP	zoqra	41532	6.____

KEY (CORRECT ANSWERS)

1. D
2. C
3. B
4. A
5. D
6. A

___

NAME AND NUMBER CHECKING

EXAMINATION SECTION
TEST 1

DIRECTIONS: This test is designed to measure your speed and accuracy. You are urged to work both quickly and accurately and to do correctly as many lists as you can in the time allowed. The test consists of lists of pairs of names and numbers. Count the number of IDENTICAL pairs in each list. Then, select the correct number, 1,2, 3, 4, or 5, and indicate your choice by circling the corresponding number on your answer paper. Two sample questions are presented for your guidance, together with the correct solutions.

SAMPLE QUESTIONS

SAMPLE LIST A

CIRCLE
CORRECT ANSWER

Adelphi College - Adelphia College
Braxton Corp. - Braxeton Corp.
Wassaic State School - Wassaic State School
Central Islip State Hospital - Central Isllip State Hospital
Greenwich House - Greenwich House

1 2 3 4 5

NOTE that there are only two correct pairs - Wassaic State School and Greenwich House. Therefore, the CORRECT answer is 2.

SAMPLE LIST B

78453694	- 78453684
784530	- 784530
533	- 534
67845	- 67845
2368745	- 2368755

1 2 3 4 5

NOTE that there are only two correct pairs - 784530 and 67845. Therefore, the CORRECT answer is 2.

LIST 1

Diagnostic Clinic	- Diagnostic Clinic
Yorkville Health	- Yorkville Health
Meinhard Clinic	- Meinhart Clinic
Corlears Clinic	- Carlears Clinic
Tremont Diagnostic	- Tremont Diagnostic

1 2 3 4 5

LIST 2

73526	- 73526
7283627198	- 7283627198
627	- 637
728352617283	- 728352617282
6281	- 6281

1 2 3 4 5

CIRCLE
CORRECT ANSWER

LIST 3

Jefferson Clinic	- Jeffersen Clinic	1 2 3 4 5
Mott Haven Center	- Mott Havan Center	
Bronx Hospital	- Bronx Hospital	
Montefiore Hospital	- Montifeore Hospital	
Beth Isreal Hospital	- Beth Israel Hospital	

LIST 4

936271826	- 936371826	1 2 3 4 5
5271	- 5291	
82637192037	- 82637192037	
527182	- 5271882	
726354256	- 72635456	

LIST 5

Trinity Hospital	- Trinity Hospital	1 2 3 4 5
Central Harlem	- Centrel Harlem	
St. Luke's Hospital	- St. Lukes' Hospital	
Mt.Sinai Hospital	- Mt.Sinia Hospital	
N.Y.Dispensery	- N.Y.Dispensary	

LIST 6

725361552637	- 725361555637	1 2 3 4 5
7526378	- 7526377	
6975	- 6975	
82637481028	- 82637481028	
3427	- 3429	

LIST 7

Misericordia Hospital	- Miseracordia Hospital	1 2 3 4 5
Lebonan Hospital	- Lebanon Hospital	
Gouverneur Hospital	- Gouverner Hospital	
German Polyclinic	- German Policlinic	
French Hospital	- French Hospital	

LIST 8

8277364933251	- 827364933351	1 2 3 4 5
63728	- 63728	
367281	- 367281	
62733846273	- 6273846293	
62836	- 6283	

LIST 9

King's County Hospital	- Kings County Hospital	1 2 3 4 5
St.Johns Long Island	- St.John's Long Island	
Bellevue Hospital	- Bellvue Hospital	
Beth David Hospital	- Beth David Hospital	
Samaritan Hospital	- Samariton Hospital	

LIST 10

		1 2 3 4 5
62836454	- 62836455	
42738267	- 42738369	
573829	- 573829	
738291627874	- 738291627874	
725	- 735	

LIST 11

		1 2 3 4 5
Bloomingdal Clinic	- Bloomingdale Clinic	
Communitty Hospital	- Community Hospital	
Metroplitan Hospital	- Metropoliton Hospital	
Lenox Hill Hospital	- Lonex Hill Hospital	
Lincoln Hospital	- Lincoln Hospital	

LIST 12

		1 2 3 4 5
6283364728	- 6283648	
627385	- 627383	
54283902	- 54283602	
63354	- 63354	
7283562781	- 7283562781	

LIST 13

		1 2 3 4 5
Sydenham Hospital	- Sydanham Hospital	
Roosevalt Hospital	- Roosevelt Hospital	
Vanderbilt Clinic	- Vanderbild Clinic	
Women's Hospital	- Woman's Hospital	
Flushing Hospital	- Flushing Hospital	

LIST 14

		1 2 3 4 5
62738	- 62738	
727355542321	- 72735542321	
263849332	- 263849332	
262837	- 263837	
47382912	- 47382922	

LIST 15

		1 2 3 4 5
Episcopal Hospital	- Episcapal Hospital	
Flower Hospital	- Flouer Hospital	
Stuyvesent Clinic	- Stuyvesant Clinic	
Jamaica Clinic	- Jamaica Clinic	
Ridgwood Clinic	- Ridgewood Clinic	

LIST 16

		1 2 3 4 5
628367299	- 628367399	
111	- 111	
118293304829	- 1182839489	
4448	- 4448	
333693678	- 333693678	

LIST 17

Arietta Crane Farm	- Areitta Crane Farm	1 2 3 4 5
Bikur Chilim Home	- Bikur Chilom Home	
Burke Foundation	- Burke Foundation	
Blythedale Home	- Blythdale Home	
Campbell Cottages	- Cambell Cottages	

LIST 18

32123	- 32132	1 2 3 4 5
273893326783	- 27389326783	
473829	- 473829	
7382937	- 7383937	
362890122332	- 36289012332	

LIST 19

Caraline Rest	- Caroline Rest	1 2 3 4 5
Loreto Rest	- Loretto Rest	
Edgewater Creche	- Edgwater Creche	
Holiday Farm	- Holiday Farm	
House of St. Giles	- House of st. Giles	

LIST 20

557286777	- 55728677	1 2 3 4 5
3678902	- 3678892	
1567839	- 1567839	
7865434712	- 7865344712	
9927382	- 9927382	

LIST 21

Isabella Home	- Isabela Home	1 2 3 4 5
James A. Moore Home	- James A. More Home	
The Robin's Nest	- The Roben's Nest	
Pelham Home	- Pelam Home	
St.Eleanora's Home	- St. Eleanora's Home	

LIST 22

273648293048	- 273648293048	1 2 3 4 5
334	- 334	
7362536478	- 7362536478	
7362819273	- 7362819273	
7362	- 7363	

LIST 23

St.Pheobe's Mission	- St.Phebe's Mission	1 2 3 4 5
Seaside Home	- Seaside Home	
Speedwell Society	- Speedwell Society	
Valeria Home	- Valera Home	
Wiltwyck	- Wildwyck	

CIRCLE
CORRECT ANSWER

LIST 24

63728	- 63738
63728192736	- 63728192738
428	- 458
62738291527	- 62738291529
63728192	- 63728192

1 2 3 4 5

LIST 25

McGaffin	- McGafin
David Ardslee	- David Ardslee
Axton Supply	- Axeton Supply Co
Alice Russell	- Alice Russell
Dobson Mfg.Co.	- Dobsen Mfg. Co.

1 2 3 4 5

———

KEY (CORRECT ANSWERS)

1.	3		11.	1
2.	3		12.	2
3.	1		13.	1
4.	1		14.	2
5.	1		15.	1
6.	2		16.	3
7.	1		17.	1
8.	2		18.	1
9.	1		19.	1
10.	2		20.	2

21.	1
22.	4
23.	2
24.	1
25.	2

———

TEST 2

DIRECTIONS: This test is designed to measure your speed and accuracy. You are urged to work both quickly and accurately and to do correctly as many lists as you can in the time allowed. The test consists of lists of pairs of names and numbers. Count the number of IDENTICAL pairs in each list. Then, select the correct number, 1, 2, 3, 4, or 5, and indicate your choice by circling the corresponding number on your answer paper. Two sample questions are presented for your guidance, together with the correct solutions.

CIRCLE
CORRECT ANSWER

LIST 1

82637381028	- 82637281028	1 2 3 4 5
928	- 928	
72937281028	- 72937281028	
7362	- 7362	
927382615	- 927382615	

LIST 2

Albee Theatre	- Albee Theatre	1 2 3 4 5
Lapland Lumber Co.	- Laplund Lumber Co.	
Adelphi College	- Adelphi College	
Jones & Son Inc.	- Jones & Sons Inc.	
S.W.Ponds Co.	- S.W. Ponds Co.	

LIST 3

85345	- 85345	1 2 3 4 5
895643278	- 895643277	
726352	- 726353	
632685	- 632685	
7263524	- 7236524	

LIST 4

Eagle Library	- Eagle Library	1 2 3 4 5
Dodge Ltd.	- Dodge Co.	
Stromberg Carlson	- Stromberg Carlsen	
Clairice Ling	- Clairice Linng	
Mason Book Co.	- Matson Book Co.	

LIST 5

66273	- 66273	1 2 3 4 5
629	- 620	
7382517283	- 7382517283	
637281	- 639281	
2738261	- 2788261	

CIRCLE
CORRECT ANSWER

LIST 6

Robert MacColl	- Robert McColl	1 2 3 4 5
Buick Motor	- Buck Motors	
Murray Bay & Co.Ltd.	- Murray Bay Co.Ltd.	
L.T. Ltyle	- L.T, Lyttle	
A.S. Landas	- A.S. Landas	

LIST 7

627152637490	- 627152637490	1 2 3 4 5
73526189	- 73526189	
5372	- 5392	
63728142	- 63728124	
4783946	- 4783046	

LIST 8

Tyndall Burke	- Tyndell Burke	1 2 3 4 5
W. Briehl	- W, Briehl	
Burritt Publishing Co.	- Buritt Publishing Co.	
Frederick Breyer & Co.	- Frederick Breyer Co.	
Bailey Buulard	- Bailey Bullard	

LIST 9

634	- 634	1 2 3 4 5
162837	- 163837	
273892223678	- 27389223678	
527182	- 527782	
3628901223	- 3629002223	

LIST 10

Ernest Boas	- Ernest Boas	1 2 3 4 5
Rankin Barne	- Rankin Barnes	
Edward Appley	- Edward Appely	
Camel	- Camel	
Caiger Food Co.	- Caiger Food Co.	

LIST 11

6273	- 6273	1 2 3 4 5
322	- 332	
15672839	- 15672839	
63728192637	- 63728192639	
738	- 738	

LIST 12

Wells Fargo Co.	- Wells Fargo Co.	1 2 3 4 5
W.D. Brett	- W.D. Britt	
Tassco Co.	- Tassko Co.	
Republic Mills	- Republic Mill	
R.W. Burnham	- R.W. Burhnam	

3 (#2)

CIRCLE
CORRECT ANSWER

LIST 13
7253529152	- 7283529152
6283	- 6383
52839102738	- 5283910238
308	- 398
82637201927	- 8263720127

1 2 3 4 5

LIST 14
Schumacker Co.	- Shumacker Co.
C.H. Caiger	- C.H. Caiger
Abraham Strauss	- Abram Straus
B.F. Boettjer	- B.F. Boettijer
Cut-Rate Store	- Cut-Rate Stores

1 2 3 4 5

LIST 15
15273826	- 15273826
72537	- 73537
726391027384	- 72639107384
637389	- 627399
725382910	- 725382910

1 2 3 4 5

LIST 16
Hixby Ltd.	- Hixby Lt'd.
S. Reiner	- S. Riener
Reynard Co.	- Reynord Co.
Esso Gassoline Co.	- Esso Gasolene Co.
Belle Brock	- Belle Brock

1 2 3 4 5

LIST 17
7245	- 7245
819263728192	- 819263728172
682537289	- 682537298
789	- 789
82936542891	- 82936542891

1 2 3 4 5

LIST 18
Joseph Cartwright	- Joseph Cartwrite
Foote Food Co.	- Foot Food Co.
Weiman & Held	- Weiman & Held
Sanderson Shoe Co.	- Sandersen Shoe Co.
A.M. Byrne	- A.N. Byrne

1 2 3 4 5

LIST 19
4738267	- 4738277
63728	- 63729
6283628901	- 6283628991
918264	- 918264
263728192037	- 2637728192073

1 2 3 4 5

CIRCLE
CORRECT ANSWER

LIST 20

Exray Laboratories	- Exray Labratories	1 2 3 4 5
Curley Toy Co.	- Curly Toy Co.	
J. Lauer & Cross	- J. Laeur & Cross	
Mireco Brands	- Mireco Brands	
Sandor Lorand	- Sandor Larand	

LIST 21

607	- 609	1 2 3 4 5
6405	- 6403	
976	- 996	
101267	- 101267	
2065432	- 20965432	

LIST 22

John Macy & Sons	- John Macy & Son	1 2 3 4 5
Venus Pencil Co.	- Venus Pencil Co,	
Nell McGinnis	- Nell McGinnis	
McCutcheon & Co.	- McCutcheon & Co.	
Sun-Tan Oil	- Sun-Tan Oil	

LIST 23

703345700	- 703345700	1 2 3 4 5
46754	- 466754	
3367490	- 3367490	
3379	- 3778	
47384	- 47394	

LIST 24

arthritis	- athritis	1 2 3 4 5
asthma	- asthma	
endocrene	- endocrene	
gastro-enterological	- gastrol-enteralogical	
orthopedic	- orthopedic	

LIST 25

743829432	- 743828432	1 2 3 4 5
998	- 998	
732816253902	- 732816252902	
46829	- 46830	
7439120249	- 7439210249	

KEY (CORRECT ANSWERS)

1.	4	11.	3
2.	3	12.	1
3.	2	13.	1
4.	1	14.	1
5.	2	15.	2
6.	1	16.	1
7.	2	17.	3
8.	1	18.	1
9.	1	19.	1
10.	3	20.	1

21.	1
22.	4
23.	2
24.	3
25.	1

———

NAME and NUMBER COMPARISONS

COMMENTARY

This test seeks to measure your ability and disposition to do a job carefully and accurately, your attention to exactness and preciseness of detail, your alertness and versatility in discerning similarities and differences between things, and your power in systematically handling written language symbols.

It is actually a test of your ability to do academic and/or clerical work, using the basic elements of verbal (qualitative) and mathematical (quantitative) learning – words and numbers.

EXAMINATION SECTION
TEST 1

Tests 1-2

DIRECTIONS: Questions 1 through 6 consist of sets of names and addresses. In each question, the name and address in Column II should be an exact copy of the name and address in Column I. *PRINT IN THE SPACE AT THE RIGHT THE LETTER:*
A. if there is a mistake only in the name
B. if there is a mistake only in the address
C. if there is a mistake in both name and address
D. if there is no mistake in either name or address

SAMPLE:

Michael Filbert   Michael Filbert
456 Reade Street   645 Reade Street
New York, N.Y. 10013   New York, N.Y. 10013

Since there is a mistake only in the address, the answer is B.

1. Esta Wong   Esta Wang   1._____
    141 West 68 St. New York,   141 West 68 St. New York,
    N.Y. 10023   N.Y. 10023

2. Dr. Alberto Grosso   Dr. Alberto Grosso   2._____
    3475 12th Avenue   3475 12th Avenue
    Brooklyn, N.Y. 11218   Brooklyn, N.Y. 11218

3. Mrs. Ruth Bortlas   Ms. Ruth Bortlas   3._____
    482 Theresa Ct.   482 Theresa Ct.
    Far Rockaway, N.Y. 11691 Far Rockaway, N.Y. 11169

4. Mr. and Mrs. Howard Fox Mr. and Mrs. Howard Fox   4._____
    2301 Sedgwick Ave.   231 Sedgwick Ave. Bronx,
    Bronx, N.Y. 10468   N.Y. 10468

5. Miss Marjorie Black   Miss Margorie Black   5._____
    223 East 23 Street   223 East 23 Street
    New York, N.Y. 10010   New York, N.Y. 10010

6. Michelle Herman   Michelle Hermann   6.___
    806 Valley Rd.   806 Valley Dr.
    Old Tappan, N.J. 07675   Old Tappan, N.J. 07675

KEY (CORRECT ANSWERS)

1. A
2. D
3. C
4. B
5. A
6. C

TEST 2

DIRECTIONS: Questions 1 through 6 consist of sets of names and addresses. In each question, the name and address in Column II should be an exact copy of the name and address in Column I. *PRINT IN THE SPACE AT THE RIGHT THE LETTER:*

A. if there is a mistake only in the name
B. if there is a mistake only in the address
C. if there is a mistake in both name and address
D. if there is no mistake in either name or address

1. Ms. Joan Kelly
   313 Franklin Ave.
   Brooklyn, N.Y. 11202

   Ms. Joan Kielly
   318 Franklin Ave.
   Brooklyn, N.Y. 11202

   1._____

2. Mrs. Eileen Engel
   47-24 86 Road
   Queens, N.Y. 11122

   Mrs. Ellen Engel
   47-24 86 Road
   Queens, N.Y. 11122

   2._____

3. Marcia Michaels
   213 E. 81 St.
   New York, N.Y. 10012

   Marcia Michaels
   213 E. 81 St.
   New York, N.Y. 10012

   3._____

4. Rev. Edward J. Smyth
   1401 Brandeis Street
   San Francisco, Calif. 96201

   Rev. Edward J. Smyth
   1401 Brandies Street
   San Francisco, Calif. 96201

   4._____

5. Alicia Rodriguez
   24-68 81 St.
   Elmhurst, N.Y. 11122

   Alicia Rodriquez
   2468 81 St.
   Elmhurst, N.Y. 11122

   5._____

6. Ernest Eisemann
   21 Columbia St.
   New York, N.Y. 10007

   Ernest Eisermann
   21 Columbia St.
   New York, N.Y. 10007

   6._____

KEY (CORRECT ANSWERS)

1. C
2. A
3. D
4. B
5. C
6. A

TEST 3

DIRECTIONS: Questions 1 through 8 consist of names, locations and telephone numbers. In each question, the name, location and number in Column II should be an exact copy of the name, location and number in Column I. *PRINT IN THE SPACE AT THE RIGHT THE LETTER:*
  A.   if there is a mistake in one line only
  B.   if there is a mistake in two lines only
  C.   if there is a mistake in three lines only
  D.   if there are no mistakes in any of the lines

1.   Ruth Lang
     EAM Bldg., Room C101
     625-2000, ext. 765

     Ruth Lang
     EAM Bldg., Room C110
     625-2000, ext. 765   1.___

2.   Anne Marie Ionozzi
     Investigations, Room 827
     576-4000, ext. 832

     Anna Marie Ionozzi
     Investigation, Room 827
     566-4000, ext. 832   2.___

3.   Willard Jameson
     Fm C Bldg. Room 687
     454-3010

     Willard Jamieson
     Fm C Bldg. Room 687
     454-3010   3.___

4.   Joanne Zimmermann
     Bldg. SW, Room 314
     532-4601

     Joanne Zimmermann
     Bldg. SW, Room 314
     532-4601   4.___

5.   Carlyle Whetstone
     Payroll Division-A, Room 212A
     262-5000, ext. 471

     Caryle Whetstone
     Payroll Division-A, Room 212A
     262-5000, ext. 417   5.___

6.   Kenneth Chiang
     Legal Council, Room 9745
     (201) 416-9100, ext. 17

     Kenneth Chiang
     Legal Counsel, Room 9745
     (201) 416-9100, ext. 17   6.___

7.   Ethel Koenig
     Personnel Services Div, Rm 433
     635-7572

     Ethel Hoenig
     Personal Services Div, Rm 433
     635-7527   7.___

8.   Joyce Ehrhardt
     Office of Administrator, Rm W56
     387-8706

     Joyce Ehrhart
     Office of Administrator, Rm W56
     387-7806   8.___

KEY (CORRECT ANSWERS)

1.	A	6.	A
2.	C	7.	C
3.	A	8.	B
4.	D		
5.	B		

———

TEST 4

DIRECTIONS: Each of questions 1 through 10 gives the identification number and name of a person who has received treatment at a certain hospital. You are to choose the option (A, B, C or D) which has EXACTLY the same number and name as those given in the question.

SAMPLE:
   123765 Frank Y. Jones
   A.   123675 Frank Y. Jones
   B.   123765 Frank T. Jones
   C.   123765 Frank Y. Johns
   D.   123765 Frank Y. Jones

The correct answer is D, because it is the only option showing the identification number and name exactly as they are in the sample question.

1.   754898 Diane Malloy   1.___

   A.   745898 Diane Malloy
   B.   754898 Dion Malloy
   C.   754898 Diane Malloy
   D.   754898 Diane Maloy

2.   661818 Ferdinand Figueroa   2.___

   A.   661818 Ferdinand Figeuroa
   B.   661618 Ferdinand Figueroa
   C.   661818 Ferdnand Figueroa
   D.   661818 Ferdinand Figueroa

3.   100101 Norman D. Braustein   3.___

   A.   100101 Norman D. Braustein
   B.   101001 Norman D. Braustein
   C.   100101 Norman P. Braustien
   D.   100101 Norman D. Bruastein

4.   838696 Robert Kittredge   4.___

   A.   838969 Robert Kittredge
   B.   838696 Robert Kittredge
   C.   388696 Robert Kittredge
   D.   838696 Robert Kittridge

5.   243716 Abraham Soletsky   5.___

   A.   243716 Abrahm Soletsky
   B.   243716 Abraham Solestky
   C.   243176 Abraham Soletsky
   D.   243716 Abraham Soletsky

6. 981121 Phillip M. Maas 6._____

    A. 981121 Phillip M. Mass
    B. 981211 Phillip M. Maas
    C. 981121 Phillip M. Maas
    D. 981121 Phillip N. Maas

7. 786556 George Macalusso 7._____

    A. 785656 George Macalusso
    B. 786556 George Macalusso
    C. 786556 George Maculusso
    D. 786556 George Macluasso

8. 639472 Eugene Weber 8._____

    A. 639472 Eugene Weber
    B. 639472 Eugene Webre
    C. 693472 Eugene Weber
    D. 639742 Eugene Weber

9. 724936 John J. Lomonaco 9._____

    A. 724936 John J. Lomanoco
    B. 724396 John L. Lomonaco
    C. 724936 John J. Lomonaco
    D. 724936 John J. Lamonaco

10. 899868 Michael Schnitzer 10._____

    A. 899868 Micheal Schnitzer
    B. 898968 Michael Schnizter
    C. 899688 Michael Schnitzer
    D. 899868 Michael Schnitzer

KEY (CORRECT ANSWERS)

1.	C		6.	C
2.	D		7.	B
3.	A		8.	A
4.	B		9.	C
5.	D		10.	D

ARITHMETIC
EXAMINATION SECTION
TEST 1

DIRECTIONS: Each question or incomplete statement is followed by several suggested answers or completions. Select the one that *BEST* answers the question or completes the statement. *PRINT THE LETTER OF TEE CORRECT ANSWER IN THE SPACE AT THE RIGHT.*

1. Add $4.34, $34.50, $6.00, $101.76, $90.67. From the result, subtract $60.54 and $10,56.   1.____
   A. $76.17   B. $156.37   C. $166.17   D. $300.37

2. Add 2,200, 2,600, 252 and 47.96. From the result, subtract 202.70, 1,200, 2,150 and   2.____
   434.43.
   A. 1,112.83   B. 1,213.46   C. 1,341.51   D. 1,348.91

3. Multiply 1850 by .05 and multiply 3300 by .08 and, then, add both results,   3.____
   A. 242.50   B. 264,00   C. 333.25   D. 356.50

4. Multiply 312.77 by .04. Round off the result to the nearest hundredth.   4.____
   A. 12.52   B. 12.511   C. 12.518   D. 12.51

5. Add 362.05, 91.13, 347.81 and 17.46 and then divide the result by 6. The answer,   5.____
   rounded off to the nearest hundredth, is:
   A. 138.409   B. 137.409   C. 136.41   D. 136.40

6. Add 66.25 and 15.06 and,then,multiply the result by 2 1/6.   6.____
   The answer is, most nearly,
   A. 176.18   B. 176.17   C. 162.66   D. 162.62

7. Each of the following items contains three decimals. In which case do *all* three decimals 7.____
   have the *SAME* value?
   A. .3; .30; .03   B. .25; .250; .2500
   C. 1.9; 1.90;1.09   D. .35; .350; .035

8. Add 1/2 the sum of (539.84 and 479.26) to 1/3 the sum of (1461.93 and 927.27). Round   8.____
   off the result to the nearest whole number.
   A. 3408   B. 2899   C. 1816   D. 1306

9. Multiply $5,906.09 by 15% and, then, divide the result by 3 and round off to the nearest   9.____
   cent.
   A. $295.30   B. $885.91   C. $2,657.74   D. $29,530.45

10. Multiply 630 by 517.   10.____
    A. 325,710   B. 345,720   C. 362,425   D. 385,660

11. Multiply 35 by 846.   11.____

   A.   4050   B.   9450   C.   18740   D.   29610

12. Multiply 823 by 0.05.   12.____

   A.   0.4115   B.   4.115   C.   41.15   D.   411.50

13. Multiply 1690 by 0.10.   13.____

   A.   0.169   B.   .1.69   C.   16.90   D.   169.0

14. Divide 2765 by 35.   14.____

   A.   71   B.   79   C.   87   D.   93

15. From $18.55 subtract $6.80.   15.____

   A. $9.75   B. $10.95   C. $11.75   D. $25.35

16. The sum of 2.75 + 4.50 + 3.60 is: 16.____

   A.   9.75   B.   10.85   C.   11.15   D.   11.95

17. The sum of 9.63 + 11.21 + 17.25 is: 17.____

   A.   36.09   B.   38.09   C.   39.92   D.   41.22

18. The sum of 112.0 + 16.9 + 3.84 is: 18.____

   A.   129.3   B.   132.74   C.   136.48   D.   167.3

19. When 65 is added to the result of 14 multiplied by 13, the answer is: 19.____

   A.   92   B.   182   C.   247   D.   16055

20. From $391.55 subtract $273.45.   20.____

   A. $118.10   B. $128.20   C. $178.10   D. $218.20

KEY (CORRECT ANSWERS)

1.	C	11.	D
2.	A	12.	C
3.	D	13.	D
4.	D	14.	B
5.	C	15.	C
6.	B	16.	B
7.	B	17.	B
8.	D	18.	B
9.	C	19.	C
10.	A	20.	A

SOLUTIONS TO PROBLEMS

1. ($4.34 + $34.50 + $6.00 + $101.76 + $90.67) - ($60.54 + $10.56) = $237.27 - $71.10 = $166.17.

2. (2200 + 2600 + 252 + 47.96) - (202.70 + 1200 + 2150 + 434.43) = 5099.96 - 3987.13 = 1112.83

3. (1850)(.05) + (3300)(.08) = 92.5 + 264 = 356.50

4. (312.77)(.04) = 12.5108 = 12.51 to nearest hundredth

5. $(362.05+91.13+347.81+17.46)\div 6 = 136.408\overline{3} = 136.41$ to nearest hundredth

6. $(66.25+15.06)(2\frac{1}{6})=176.171\overline{6} \approx 176.17$

7. .25 = .250 = .2500

8. $(\frac{1}{2})(539.84+479.26)+\frac{1}{3}(1461.93+927.27)$ = 509.55 + 796.4 = 1305.95 = 1306 nearest whole number

9. ($5906.09)(.15) ÷ 3 = ($885.9135)/3 = 295.3045 = $295.30 to nearest cent

10. (630)(517) = 325,710

11. (35)(846) = 29,610

12. (823)(.05) = 41.15

13. (1690)(10) = 169.0

14. 2765÷3.5 = 79

15. $18.55 - $6.80 = $11.75

16. 2.75 + 4.50 + 3.60 = 10.85

17. 9.63 + 11.21 + 17.25 = 38.09

18. 112.0 + 16.9 + 3.84 = 132.74

19. 65 + (14)(13) = 65 + 182 = 247

20. $391.55 - $273.45 = $118.10

———

TEST 2

DIRECTIONS Each question or incomplete statement is followed by several suggested answers or completions. Select the one that *BEST* answers the question or completes the statement. *PRINT THE LETTER OF TEE CORRECT ANSWER IN THE SPACE AT THE RIGHT.*

1. The sum of $29.61 + $101.53 + $943.64 is: 1.____
   A. $983.88   B. $1074.78   C. $1174.98   D. $1341.42

2. The sum of $132.25 + $85.63 + $7056,44 is: 2.____
   A. $1694.19   B. $7274.32   C. $8464.57   D. $9346.22

3. The sum of 4010 + 1271 + 838 + 23 is: 3.____
   A. 6142   B. 6162   C. 6242   D. 6362

4. The sum of 53632 + 27403 + 98765 + 75424 is: 4.____
   A. 19214   B. 215214   C. 235224   D. 255224

5. The sum of 76342 + 49050 + 21206 + 59989 is: 5.____
   A. 196586   B. 206087   C. 206587   D. 234487

6. The sum of $452.13 + $963.45 + $621.25 is: 6.____
   A. $1936.83   B. $2036.83   C. $2095.73   D. $2135.73

7. The sum of 36392 + 42156 + 98765 is: 7.____
   A. 167214   B. 177203   C. 177313   D. 178213

8. The sum of 40125 + 87123 + 24689 is: 8.____
   A. 141827   B. 151827   C. 151937   D. 161947

9. The sum of 2379 + 4015 + 6521 + 9986 is: 9.____
   A. 22901   B. 22819   C. 21801   D. 21791

10. From 50962 subtract 36197. 10.____
    A. 14675   B. 14765   C. 14865   D. 24765

11. From 90000 subtract 31928. 11.____
    A. 58072   B. 59062   C. 68172   D. 69182

12. From 63764 subtract 21548. 12.____
    A. 42216   B. 43122   C. 45126   D. 85312

13. From $9605.13 subtract $2715.96. 13.____
    A. $12,321.09   B. $8,690.16   C. $6,990.07   D. $6,889.17

14. From 76421 subtract 73101.   14.____

    A. 3642   B. 3540   C. 3320   D. 3242

15. From $8.25 subtract $6.50.   15.____

    A. $1.25   B. $1.50   C. $1.75   D. $2.25

16. Multiply 583 by 0.50.   16.____

    A. $291.50   B. 28.15   C. 2.815   D. 0.2815

17. Multiply 0.35 by 1045.   17.____

    A. 0.36575   B. 3.6575   C. 36.575   D. 365.75

18. Multiply 25 by 2513.   18.____

    A. 62825   B. 62725   C. 60825   D. 52825

19. Multiply 423 by 0.01.   19.____

    A. 0.0423   B. 0.423   C. 4.23   D. 42.3

20. Multiply 6.70 by 3.2.   20.____

    A. 2.1440   B. 21.440   C. 214.40   D. 2144.0

———

KEY (CORRECT ANSWERS)

1.	B	11.	A
2.	B	12.	A
3.	A	13.	D
4.	D	14.	C
5.	C	15.	C
6.	B	16.	A
7.	C	17.	D
8.	C	18.	A
9.	A	19.	C
10.	B	20.	B

———

SOLUTIONS TO PROBLEMS

1. $29.61 + $101.53 + $943.64 = $1074.78

2. $132.25 + $85.63 + $7056.44 = $7274.32

3. 4010 + 1271 + 838 + 23 = 6142

4. 53,632 + 27,103 + 98,765 + 75,424 = 255,224

5. 76,342 + 49,050 + 21,206 + 59,989 = 206,587

6. $452.13 + $963.45 + $621.25 = $2036.83

7. 36,392 + 42,156 + 98,765 = 177,313

8. 40,125 + 87,123 + 24,689 = 151,937

9. 2379 + 4015 + 6521 + 9986 = 22,901

10. 50962 - 36197 = 14,765

11. 90,000 - 31,928 = 58,072

12. 63,764 - 21,548 = 42,216

13. $9605.13 - $2715.96 = $6889.17

14. 76,421 - 73,101 = 3320

15. $8.25 - $6.50 = $1.75

16. (583)(.50) = 291.50

17. (.35)(1045) = 365.75

18. (25)(2513) = 62,825

19. (423)(.01) = 4.23

20. (6.70)(3.2) = 21.44

———

TEST 3

DIRECTIONS : Each question or incomplete statement is followed by several suggested answers or completions. Select the one that *BEST* answers the question or completes the statement. *PRINT THE LETTER OF TEE CORRECT ANSWER IN THE SPACE AT THE RIGHT.*

Questions 1-4.

DIRECTIONS: For each of Questions 1-4, perform the indicated arithmetic and choose the correct answer from among the four choices given.

1. 12.485
    + 347
    _____

    A. 12,038   B. 12,128   C. 12,782   D. 12,832   1._____

2. 74,137
    + 711
    _____

    A. 74,326   B. 74,848   C. 78,028   D. .D. 78,926   2._____

3. 3,749
    - 671
    _____

    A. 3,078   B. 3,168   C. 4,028   D. 4,420   3._____

4. 19,805
    -18904
    _____

    A. 109   B. 901   C. 1,109   D. 1,901   4._____

5. When 119 is subtracted from the sum of 2016 + 1634, the remainder is: 5._____
    A. 2460   B. 3531   C. 3650   D. 3769

6. Multiply 35 X 65 X 15.   6._____
    A. 2275   B. 24265   C. 31145   D. 34125

7. 90% expressed as a decimal is: 7._____
    A. .009   B. .09   C. .9   D. 9.0

8. Seven-tenths of a foot expressed in inches is: 8._____
    A. 5.5   B. 6.5   C. 7   D. 8.4

9. If 95 men were divided into crews of five men each, the *number* of crews that will be   9._____
    formed is:
    A. 16   B. 17   C. 18   D. 19

10. If a man earns $19.50 an hour, the *number* of working hours it will take him to earn $4,875 is, most nearly,

    A. 225   B. 250   C. 275   D. 300

10.___

11. If 5 1/2 loads of gravel cost $55.00, then 6 1/2 loads will cost:

    A. $60.   B. $62.50   C. $65.   D. $66.00

11.___

12. At $2.50 a yard, 27 yards of concrete will cost:

    A. $36.   B. $41.80   C. $54.   D. $67.50

12.___

13. A distance is measured and found to be 52.23 feet. In feet and inches, this distance is, most nearly, 52 feet *and*

    A. 2 3/4"   B. 3 1/4"   C. 3 3/4"   D. 4 1/4"

13.___

14. If a maintainer gets $5.20 per hour and time and one-half for working over 40 hours, his *gross* salary for a week in which he worked 43 hours would be

    A. $208.00   B. $223.60   C. $231.40   D. $335.40

14.___

15. The circumference of a circle is given by the formula $C = \Pi D$, where C is the circumference, D is the diameter, and Π is about 3 1/7.
If a coil is 15 turns of steel cable has an average diameter of 20 inches, the *total* length of cable on the coil is *nearest to*

    A. 5 feet   B. 78 feet   C. 550 feet   D. 943 feet

15.___

16. The measurements of a poured concrete foundation show that 54 cubic feet of concrete have been placed.
If payment for this concrete is to be on the basis of cubic yards, the 54 cubic feet must be

    A. multiplied by 27   B. multiplied by 3
    C. divided by 27   D. divided by 3

16.___

17. If the cost of 4 1/2 tons of structural steel is $1,800, then the cost of 12 tons is, most nearly,

    A. $4,800   B. $5,400   C. $7,200   D. $216,000

17.___

18. An hourly-paid employee working 12:00 midnight to 8:00 a.m. is directed to report to the medical staff for a physical examination at 11:00 a.m. of the same day.
The pay allowed him for reporting will be an extra

    A. 1 hour   B. 2 hours   C. 3 hours   D. 4 hours

18.___

19. The *total* length of four pieces of 2" pipe, whose lengths are 7' 3 1/2" , 4' 2 3/16", 5' 7 5/16", and 8' 5 7/8", respectively, is:

    A. 24' 6 3/4"   B. 24' 7 15/16"
    C. 25' 5 13/16"   D. 25' 6 7/8"

19.___

20. As a senior mortuary caretaker, you are preparing a monthly report, using the following figures:

No. of bodies received	983
No. of bodies claimed	720
No. of bodies sent to city cemetery	14
No. of bodies sent to medical schools	9

    How many bodies remained at the end of the monthly reporting period?

    20.____

    A.   230   B.   240   C.   250   D.   260

    ———

KEY (CORRECT ANSWERS)

1.	D	11.	C
2.	B	12.	D
3.	A	13.	A
4.	B	14.	C
5.	B	15.	B
6.	D	16.	C
7.	C	17.	A
8.	D	18.	C
9.	D	19.	D
10.	B	20.	B

———

SOLUTIONS TO PROBLEMS

1. $12,485 + 347 = 12,832$

2. $74,137 + 711 = 74,848$

3. $3749 - 671 = 3078$

4. $19,805 - 18,904 = 901$

5. $(2016 + 1634) - 119 = 3650 - 119 = 3531$

6. $(35)(65)(15) = 34,125$

7. $90\% = .90$ or $.9$

8. $(\frac{7}{10})(12) = 8.4$ inches

9. $95 \div 5 = 19$ crews

10. $\$4875 \div \$19.50 = 250$ days

11. Let x = cost. Then, $\dfrac{5\frac{1}{2}}{6\frac{1}{2}} = \dfrac{\$55.00}{x}$. $5\frac{1}{2} = 357.50$. Solving, x = $65

12. $(\$2.50)(27) = \$67.50$

13. $.23\text{-ft.} = 2.76\text{in.}$, so $52.23\text{ft} \approx 52\,\text{ft.}\,2\frac{3}{4}\text{in.}$ $(.76 \approx \frac{3}{4})$

14. Salary = $(\$5.20)(40) + (\$7.80)(3) = \$231.40$

15. Length $\approx (15)(3\frac{1}{7})(20) \approx 943$ in. ≈ 78 ft.

16. There are 27 cu.ft. in 1 cu.yd. To change from 54 cu.ft. to cu.yds., divide by 27.

17. $\$1800 \div 4\frac{1}{2} = = \$400$ per ton. Then, 12 tons cost $(\$400)(12) = \$4800$

18. Instead of working 12 to 8, he will be staying until 11 AM, an extra 3 hours.

19. $7'3\frac{1}{2}" + 4'2\frac{3}{16}" + 5'7\frac{5}{16}" + 8'5\frac{7}{8}" = 24'17\frac{30}{16}" = 24'18\frac{7}{8}"$

20. $983 - 720 - 14 - 9 = 240$ bodies left.

POLICE SCIENCE NOTES

COLLECTION, IDENTIFICATION AND PRESERVATION OF EVIDENCE

The Definition and importance of Evidence

Definition

Evidence can be defined as "any medium of proof or probative matter, legally presented at the trial of any issue, by the participants of the trial and through the medium of witnesses, records, documents, objects, etc., for the purpose of inducing belief in the minds of the court and the jurors as to its creditability and contention." In more general terms, evidence is anything that can be legally presented to indicate the guilt of a criminal act or to aid in determining the truth about any fact in question.

Importance

The primary importance of evidence is the aid it offers in the identification of the guilty party and in his successful prosecution. Because of this, the proper collection, identification, and preservation of evidence make up a vital part of police operations. Cases may be won or lost depending upon the proficiency of the police department in this area.

Evidence is the means by which the patrolman or investigator can aid the prosecutor in giving the court a complete picture of the crime and its commission. It explains the facts that the officer uses to determine that the accused is guilty. Properly prepared and presented, evidence may serve the same purpose as taking the court and the jury to the scene of the crime and reconstructing the events which led to the commission of the crime charged.

In order to insure that this vital function is performed properly, most departments have specialists known as criminal investigators to collect, search and properly evaluate evidence. The reason for this is that such specialization saves time and leaves the patrolman free to resume his primary duties once the investigator arrives at the scene. However, since the general patrolman or the auxiliary policeman will usually be the first to arrive at the scene and therefore is crucial to the outcome of the criminal investigation, it is important that they have an adequate understanding of evidence and be skilled in its preservation and protection. The need for developing adequate investigative skills is especially crucial in those departments without a specialist and where the officers are expected to conduct their own investigation.

Classification of Evidence

Evidence may be divided into three major classifications:

DIRECT evidence directly establishes the main fact of issue. It applies immediately to the fact to be proven or disproven and is usually what a person sees, hears, or knows.

CIRCUMSTANTIAL evidence tends to prove or disprove the fact in issue by other facts leading to a presumption of the truth or falsity of the main fact. The essence here is inference-establishing a factor or circumstance from which a court may infer another fact. It may be real evidence or things which may be said to "speak for themselves." Ownership of the murder weapon, the fingerprints thereon, and the inability of the accused to account for his actions at the time of the crime would be matters of circumstantial evidence.

REAL OR PHYSICAL evidence comprises those tangible objects introduced at the trial which speak for themselves and need no explanation, just identification. Examples of real evidence would be guns, fingerprints, and bloodstains. Real evidence can be further divided into:

FIXED OR IMMOVABLE evidence which by its very nature cannot be moved from the crime scene. It includes such objects as latent fingerprints, tool marks, doors, windows, wall plaster, etc. Of course, fingerprints may be lifted, casts made of foot and tire marks, and photographs taken of the entire scene; but the actual object remains incapable of being transported to the courtroom.

MOVABLE evidence which can be preserved intact for examination at headquarters and presentation in the courtroom. This includes such objects as bullets, tools, hair, documents, clothing, and many other similar objects.

Chain of Custody - The Cardinal Rule of Evidence

In order for the evidence to be properly admitted into court, its location and holder must be accurately established from the time the officer or investigator finds the evidence until it is presented in court. If the whereabouts of the evidence cannot be established, even for a moment, the court will rule it is inadmissible. The reason for this is because if it can be shown that the evidence was out of responsible hands or unaccountable for, then it is also likely that the evidence could have been tampered with thereby negating its validity and leaving the court no alternative but to dismiss it. Therefore, in order to overcome the questions presented by the defense and to impress the judge and jury that the evidence has been properly protected, the police officer must establish an accurate "chain of custody" for each piece of evidence presented in court.

Perhaps the best method of maintaining an accurate chain of custody is through the use of receipts. If the evidence is to be out of the officer's hand for even a minute he should demand a receipt containing: the time, date, and place where the exchange occurred, to whom the evidence was given, and for what purpose. Likewise, if the officer receives any evidence for transportation or for other purposes he should fill out and give a receipt to the person giving him the evidence.

Collection of Evidence

Two points to be remembered by all personnel concerned with the collection of evidence are: (1) there, is rarely a major crime committed without some kind of evidence being left at the scene, and (2) nothing at a crime scene is too significant to be overlooked. The ultimate success of any investigation will depend on the acumen of the officers in searching the scene, recognizing evidence, and preserving it.

Preliminary Activities at the Crime Scene

The first officer at the crime scene who will usually be either the beat patrolman or the auxiliary policeman should:

1. Assist the injured when necessary.
2. Notify the proper experts and equipment to conduct a proper crime scene examination.
3. Obtain pertinent data from the witnesses and any suspects, keeping them separated if possible.
4. Use the most effective means possible to protect the crime scene from any intrusions by unauthorized personnel.
5. Arrest any perpetrators caught at or near the scene.
6. Assist the investigator when he arrives to examine the scene.

The investigator or whoever is in charge of the investigation should determine from the initial officer what has been done and what needs to be done before taking command of the situation. He will then conduct a thorough investigation of the scene and question all witnesses, victims, and suspects at the scene.

Examination of the Crime Scene

Usually the first person to be admitted to the crime scene is the photographer who will take as many photographs as necessary to insure proper coverage of the scene for further study and analysis. While the photographer is shooting the scene, the investigator will make a sketch of the scene to supplement the photographs by adding the dimensions of height, distances, and locations of the scene. Notes should also be made of the camera's position, characteristics, and the weather conditions that affect the camera's settings.

The next step in the process is the search of the crime scene area which presents various problems, especially when the area is extensive. It is essential that proper consideration be given to all aspects of the search problems before proceeding, in order that the search can be made as complete and as thorough as possible. The general organization of the search party will be determined by the size and type of the area to be covered, available personnel, and the equipment with which the party must work. It is important that the search party be divided into manageable units with each unit aware of just what area it is responsible for searching.

The number of men necessary to conduct a search will largely depends on the conditions existing at the time. Search parties may consist of as many as a hundred men, but should never be less than two. Regardless of how many people conduct the search, a careful and methodical effort must be exerted, the search should proceed according to plan, and the searchers should search for one thing at a time. If the search is going to be for fingerprints then the search should be for fingerprints only until they are all found or there is good reason to believe that there are none. Then the search can be for bloodstains or hair, and so on down the line. The searchers may note the presence and location of one piece of evidence while looking for another piece, but the evidence noted should not be touched until the searchers are specifically looking for it. It is also a good practice to have each man responsible for a particular duty during the search. He can be a note taker, sketcher, evidence collector, or whatever else is necessary. Then when the search starts again he should be switched to another duty. This helps keep the persons alert, and insure adequate coverage of the scene. Never search a crime scene just once; always go over and over the scene until everyone is satisfied that all the evidence has been found. However, do not handle evidence more than is necessary.

The Identification of Evidence

To insure the proper chain of custody of any evidence found during the search it is necessary that every piece of evidence be marked for identification by the person who found it. Others who witness its finding should also mark the evidence of witness. If the evidence does not provide sufficient suitable area for more than a single mark it should be marked by the finding officer and witnessed by other persons. The characteristics of the mark should be recorded in the notes of the officer as well as the witnesses.

The following steps should be followed in the marking of any evidence:

1. Each bit of evidence should be appropriately marked at the time it is removed from its original position. No piece of evidence should be removed from the position in which it was found until after it has been photographed, sketched, processed for latent fingerprints, and listed in the investigator's notebook.

2. The mark "X" should never be used to identify evidence. The identifying mark should be one that is characteristic and easily identifiable. Using the written initials of the finder is considered best. The mark used and its position as well as any serial numbers or distinctive marks present on the object should be recorded in the officer's notebook for further reference.

3. Whenever possible mark the object itself, taking extreme care to prevent any destruction of the value of the evidence. Unless evidence or the article itself prohibits it, the marks made on all articles of a similar nature should be in the same direction.

4. Always mark the container in which the object is being placed as well as the object. If the object cannot be marked then seal the container and mark the seal as well as the container.

Proper marking and the keeping of notes on the evidence found during the course of an investigation will make it possible for the officer to positively identify each piece of evidence at the time it is presented in court. Using a mark which is characteristic and one that will not have been accidentally placed on the evidence, as well as knowing just where to locate the mark on the evidence is of great value to the officer witness. He will be poised and confident in his manner of handling the evidence and the judge and jury will be more impressed as to the value of the evidence presented.

Preservation and transportation of Evidence Preservation

Each article of evidence should be placed in an appropriate container depending on the nature and size of the evidence. It is recommended that the container used should be larger than necessary to normally accommodate the evidence article, so as to prevent it from being crushed or squeezed by other articles. However, the container should not be so large as to cause damage to the evidence from excessive movement. The containers should be new and clean and each article of evidence should be packed in a separate container. This is especially necessary where evidence might have foreign matter adhering to it. Should any matter adhering to the evidence fall or become separated from the article during or after packing, it will be found in the container in which the article was packed.

Transporting the Article

The transportation of the sealed evidence to the laboratory should be accompanied by the officer who collected the evidence. It has to be shipped to a laboratory, the safest and most practical method of delivery should be used and in the case of perishables, the speediest method possible should be employed.

The contents of any container should be clearly listed on the package or label. If several individual packages are packed into a single large container, the larger container should be labeled to show the content of the individual containers. This would be in addition to the labels on the individual containers. The information contained on the package should include: (1) contents of the package, (2) name of the person from whom the property was taken or where it was found, (3) the number of the case on which the evidence has a bearing, (4) the date and time it was found, (5) the name of the officer who found or received it and (6) the article to be subjected to laboratory examination, and (7) the type of examination suggested.

Storage of Evidence

One of the most important phases of maintaining the value of the evidence is its storage. The evidence must be stored in such a manner that there is no question as to actual possession.

In some departments the officer has to store the evidence in his personal locker, in others, special wall lockers are set aside for the storage of evidence with keys only available to the officer in charge of each watch and the officer who has evidence to store.

Probably the best arrangement would be for the department to have a property room with an officer from each watch in charge. After obtaining evidence the officer could then place it in the property room and receive a receipt for it. This room should have the proper facilities for storing evidence along with a strict security apparatus to keep all people except the officer of each watch in charge of it from entering.

This way the evidence could be properly stored according to its needs and the officer can be assured that the evidence has been under strict control and carefully guarded until it is needed in the laboratory or in the courtroom. He can then maintain the chain of evidence and assure the court and jury the evidence was given the best of care and handled by responsible personnel.

Conclusion

The identification, collection, and preservation of evidence are of crucial importance to the execution of police responsibilities. The auxiliary policeman will be expected to take part in these duties when the occasion arises. His specific duties will naturally depend upon the department with which he is allied. However, in most departments because of the presence of specialists in the area of criminal investigation his main duties will be the protection of the scene and assisting the specialists where necessary. Regardless of what his duties are, the auxiliary policeman should constantly strive to gain further knowledge about this field for his own benefit. In a natural or manmade disaster he may be the only representative of the law left within an entire area and, at that time, his knowledge of proper investigative techniques will help continue law and order in society.

The auxiliary officer should remember that there are always clues at a crime scene and that everything within a crime scene is significant. Only knowledge, experience, and patience will bring these clues into the open and these take time to develop. He should never forget the importance of maintaining the chain of custody by issuing and receiving receipts. Above all, he should be constantly aware of the importance of evidence and should constantly try to improve his own skills in its identification, collection, and preservation.

———

ANSWER SHEET

TEST NO. _____ PART _____ TITLE OF POSITION _____

(AS GIVEN IN EXAMINATION ANNOUNCEMENT - INCLUDE OPTION, IF ANY)

PLACE OF EXAMINATION _____ DATE_____

(CITY OR TOWN)   (STATE)

RATING

USE THE SPECIAL PENCIL.   MAKE GLOSSY BLACK MARKS.

	A B C D E		A B C D E		A B C D E		A B C D E		A B C D E
1	∷ ∷ ∷ ∷ ∷	26	∷ ∷ ∷ ∷ ∷	51	∷ ∷ ∷ ∷ ∷	76	∷ ∷ ∷ ∷ ∷	101	∷ ∷ ∷ ∷ ∷
2	∷ ∷ ∷ ∷ ∷	27	∷ ∷ ∷ ∷ ∷	52	∷ ∷ ∷ ∷ ∷	77	∷ ∷ ∷ ∷ ∷	102	∷ ∷ ∷ ∷ ∷
3	∷ ∷ ∷ ∷ ∷	28	∷ ∷ ∷ ∷ ∷	53	∷ ∷ ∷ ∷ ∷	78	∷ ∷ ∷ ∷ ∷	103	∷ ∷ ∷ ∷ ∷
4	∷ ∷ ∷ ∷ ∷	29	∷ ∷ ∷ ∷ ∷	54	∷ ∷ ∷ ∷ ∷	79	∷ ∷ ∷ ∷ ∷	104	∷ ∷ ∷ ∷ ∷
5	∷ ∷ ∷ ∷ ∷	30	∷ ∷ ∷ ∷ ∷	55	∷ ∷ ∷ ∷ ∷	80	∷ ∷ ∷ ∷ ∷	105	∷ ∷ ∷ ∷ ∷
6	∷ ∷ ∷ ∷ ∷	31	∷ ∷ ∷ ∷ ∷	56	∷ ∷ ∷ ∷ ∷	81	∷ ∷ ∷ ∷ ∷	106	∷ ∷ ∷ ∷ ∷
7	∷ ∷ ∷ ∷ ∷	32	∷ ∷ ∷ ∷ ∷	57	∷ ∷ ∷ ∷ ∷	82	∷ ∷ ∷ ∷ ∷	107	∷ ∷ ∷ ∷ ∷
8	∷ ∷ ∷ ∷ ∷	33	∷ ∷ ∷ ∷ ∷	58	∷ ∷ ∷ ∷ ∷	83	∷ ∷ ∷ ∷ ∷	108	∷ ∷ ∷ ∷ ∷
9	∷ ∷ ∷ ∷ ∷	34	∷ ∷ ∷ ∷ ∷	59	∷ ∷ ∷ ∷ ∷	84	∷ ∷ ∷ ∷ ∷	109	∷ ∷ ∷ ∷ ∷
10	∷ ∷ ∷ ∷ ∷	35	∷ ∷ ∷ ∷ ∷	60	∷ ∷ ∷ ∷ ∷	85	∷ ∷ ∷ ∷ ∷	110	∷ ∷ ∷ ∷ ∷

Make only ONE mark for each answer.   Additional and stray marks may be counted as mistakes.   In making corrections, erase errors COMPLETELY.

	A B C D E		A B C D E		A B C D E		A B C D E		A B C D E
11	∷ ∷ ∷ ∷ ∷	36	∷ ∷ ∷ ∷ ∷	61	∷ ∷ ∷ ∷ ∷	86	∷ ∷ ∷ ∷ ∷	111	∷ ∷ ∷ ∷ ∷
12	∷ ∷ ∷ ∷ ∷	37	∷ ∷ ∷ ∷ ∷	62	∷ ∷ ∷ ∷ ∷	87	∷ ∷ ∷ ∷ ∷	112	∷ ∷ ∷ ∷ ∷
13	∷ ∷ ∷ ∷ ∷	38	∷ ∷ ∷ ∷ ∷	63	∷ ∷ ∷ ∷ ∷	88	∷ ∷ ∷ ∷ ∷	113	∷ ∷ ∷ ∷ ∷
14	∷ ∷ ∷ ∷ ∷	39	∷ ∷ ∷ ∷ ∷	64	∷ ∷ ∷ ∷ ∷	89	∷ ∷ ∷ ∷ ∷	114	∷ ∷ ∷ ∷ ∷
15	∷ ∷ ∷ ∷ ∷	40	∷ ∷ ∷ ∷ ∷	65	∷ ∷ ∷ ∷ ∷	90	∷ ∷ ∷ ∷ ∷	115	∷ ∷ ∷ ∷ ∷
16	∷ ∷ ∷ ∷ ∷	41	∷ ∷ ∷ ∷ ∷	66	∷ ∷ ∷ ∷ ∷	91	∷ ∷ ∷ ∷ ∷	116	∷ ∷ ∷ ∷ ∷
17	∷ ∷ ∷ ∷ ∷	42	∷ ∷ ∷ ∷ ∷	67	∷ ∷ ∷ ∷ ∷	92	∷ ∷ ∷ ∷ ∷	117	∷ ∷ ∷ ∷ ∷
18	∷ ∷ ∷ ∷ ∷	43	∷ ∷ ∷ ∷ ∷	68	∷ ∷ ∷ ∷ ∷	93	∷ ∷ ∷ ∷ ∷	118	∷ ∷ ∷ ∷ ∷
19	∷ ∷ ∷ ∷ ∷	44	∷ ∷ ∷ ∷ ∷	69	∷ ∷ ∷ ∷ ∷	94	∷ ∷ ∷ ∷ ∷	119	∷ ∷ ∷ ∷ ∷
20	∷ ∷ ∷ ∷ ∷	45	∷ ∷ ∷ ∷ ∷	70	∷ ∷ ∷ ∷ ∷	95	∷ ∷ ∷ ∷ ∷	120	∷ ∷ ∷ ∷ ∷
21	∷ ∷ ∷ ∷ ∷	46	∷ ∷ ∷ ∷ ∷	71	∷ ∷ ∷ ∷ ∷	96	∷ ∷ ∷ ∷ ∷	121	∷ ∷ ∷ ∷ ∷
22	∷ ∷ ∷ ∷ ∷	47	∷ ∷ ∷ ∷ ∷	72	∷ ∷ ∷ ∷ ∷	97	∷ ∷ ∷ ∷ ∷	122	∷ ∷ ∷ ∷ ∷
23	∷ ∷ ∷ ∷ ∷	48	∷ ∷ ∷ ∷ ∷	73	∷ ∷ ∷ ∷ ∷	98	∷ ∷ ∷ ∷ ∷	123	∷ ∷ ∷ ∷ ∷
24	∷ ∷ ∷ ∷ ∷	49	∷ ∷ ∷ ∷ ∷	74	∷ ∷ ∷ ∷ ∷	99	∷ ∷ ∷ ∷ ∷	124	∷ ∷ ∷ ∷ ∷
25	∷ ∷ ∷ ∷ ∷	50	∷ ∷ ∷ ∷ ∷	75	∷ ∷ ∷ ∷ ∷	100	∷ ∷ ∷ ∷ ∷	125	∷ ∷ ∷ ∷ ∷

ANSWER SHEET

TEST NO. _____ PART _____ TITLE OF POSITION _____

(AS GIVEN IN EXAMINATION ANNOUNCEMENT - INCLUDE OPTION, IF ANY)

PLACE OF EXAMINATION _____ DATE _____

(CITY OR TOWN)   (STATE)

RATING

USE THE SPECIAL PENCIL.   MAKE GLOSSY BLACK MARKS.

	A B C D E		A B C D E		A B C D E		A B C D E		A B C D E
1	‖ ‖ ‖ ‖ ‖	26	‖ ‖ ‖ ‖ ‖	51	‖ ‖ ‖ ‖ ‖	76	‖ ‖ ‖ ‖ ‖	101	‖ ‖ ‖ ‖ ‖
2	‖ ‖ ‖ ‖ ‖	27	‖ ‖ ‖ ‖ ‖	52	‖ ‖ ‖ ‖ ‖	77	‖ ‖ ‖ ‖ ‖	102	‖ ‖ ‖ ‖ ‖
3	‖ ‖ ‖ ‖ ‖	28	‖ ‖ ‖ ‖ ‖	53	‖ ‖ ‖ ‖ ‖	78	‖ ‖ ‖ ‖ ‖	103	‖ ‖ ‖ ‖ ‖
4	‖ ‖ ‖ ‖ ‖	29	‖ ‖ ‖ ‖ ‖	54	‖ ‖ ‖ ‖ ‖	79	‖ ‖ ‖ ‖ ‖	104	‖ ‖ ‖ ‖ ‖
5	‖ ‖ ‖ ‖ ‖	30	‖ ‖ ‖ ‖ ‖	55	‖ ‖ ‖ ‖ ‖	80	‖ ‖ ‖ ‖ ‖	105	‖ ‖ ‖ ‖ ‖
6	‖ ‖ ‖ ‖ ‖	31	‖ ‖ ‖ ‖ ‖	56	‖ ‖ ‖ ‖ ‖	81	‖ ‖ ‖ ‖ ‖	106	‖ ‖ ‖ ‖ ‖
7	‖ ‖ ‖ ‖ ‖	32	‖ ‖ ‖ ‖ ‖	57	‖ ‖ ‖ ‖ ‖	82	‖ ‖ ‖ ‖ ‖	107	‖ ‖ ‖ ‖ ‖
8	‖ ‖ ‖ ‖ ‖	33	‖ ‖ ‖ ‖ ‖	58	‖ ‖ ‖ ‖ ‖	83	‖ ‖ ‖ ‖ ‖	108	‖ ‖ ‖ ‖ ‖
9	‖ ‖ ‖ ‖ ‖	34	‖ ‖ ‖ ‖ ‖	59	‖ ‖ ‖ ‖ ‖	84	‖ ‖ ‖ ‖ ‖	109	‖ ‖ ‖ ‖ ‖
10	‖ ‖ ‖ ‖ ‖	35	‖ ‖ ‖ ‖ ‖	60	‖ ‖ ‖ ‖ ‖	85	‖ ‖ ‖ ‖ ‖	110	‖ ‖ ‖ ‖ ‖

Make only ONE mark for each answer.   Additional and stray marks may be
counted as mistakes.   In making corrections, erase errors COMPLETELY.

	A B C D E		A B C D E		A B C D E		A B C D E		A B C D E
11	‖ ‖ ‖ ‖ ‖	36	‖ ‖ ‖ ‖ ‖	61	‖ ‖ ‖ ‖ ‖	86	‖ ‖ ‖ ‖ ‖	111	‖ ‖ ‖ ‖ ‖
12	‖ ‖ ‖ ‖ ‖	37	‖ ‖ ‖ ‖ ‖	62	‖ ‖ ‖ ‖ ‖	87	‖ ‖ ‖ ‖ ‖	112	‖ ‖ ‖ ‖ ‖
13	‖ ‖ ‖ ‖ ‖	38	‖ ‖ ‖ ‖ ‖	63	‖ ‖ ‖ ‖ ‖	88	‖ ‖ ‖ ‖ ‖	113	‖ ‖ ‖ ‖ ‖
14	‖ ‖ ‖ ‖ ‖	39	‖ ‖ ‖ ‖ ‖	64	‖ ‖ ‖ ‖ ‖	89	‖ ‖ ‖ ‖ ‖	114	‖ ‖ ‖ ‖ ‖
15	‖ ‖ ‖ ‖ ‖	40	‖ ‖ ‖ ‖ ‖	65	‖ ‖ ‖ ‖ ‖	90	‖ ‖ ‖ ‖ ‖	115	‖ ‖ ‖ ‖ ‖
16	‖ ‖ ‖ ‖ ‖	41	‖ ‖ ‖ ‖ ‖	66	‖ ‖ ‖ ‖ ‖	91	‖ ‖ ‖ ‖ ‖	116	‖ ‖ ‖ ‖ ‖
17	‖ ‖ ‖ ‖ ‖	42	‖ ‖ ‖ ‖ ‖	67	‖ ‖ ‖ ‖ ‖	92	‖ ‖ ‖ ‖ ‖	117	‖ ‖ ‖ ‖ ‖
18	‖ ‖ ‖ ‖ ‖	43	‖ ‖ ‖ ‖ ‖	68	‖ ‖ ‖ ‖ ‖	93	‖ ‖ ‖ ‖ ‖	118	‖ ‖ ‖ ‖ ‖
19	‖ ‖ ‖ ‖ ‖	44	‖ ‖ ‖ ‖ ‖	69	‖ ‖ ‖ ‖ ‖	94	‖ ‖ ‖ ‖ ‖	119	‖ ‖ ‖ ‖ ‖
20	‖ ‖ ‖ ‖ ‖	45	‖ ‖ ‖ ‖ ‖	70	‖ ‖ ‖ ‖ ‖	95	‖ ‖ ‖ ‖ ‖	120	‖ ‖ ‖ ‖ ‖
21	‖ ‖ ‖ ‖ ‖	46	‖ ‖ ‖ ‖ ‖	71	‖ ‖ ‖ ‖ ‖	96	‖ ‖ ‖ ‖ ‖	121	‖ ‖ ‖ ‖ ‖
22	‖ ‖ ‖ ‖ ‖	47	‖ ‖ ‖ ‖ ‖	72	‖ ‖ ‖ ‖ ‖	97	‖ ‖ ‖ ‖ ‖	122	‖ ‖ ‖ ‖ ‖
23	‖ ‖ ‖ ‖ ‖	48	‖ ‖ ‖ ‖ ‖	73	‖ ‖ ‖ ‖ ‖	98	‖ ‖ ‖ ‖ ‖	123	‖ ‖ ‖ ‖ ‖
24	‖ ‖ ‖ ‖ ‖	49	‖ ‖ ‖ ‖ ‖	74	‖ ‖ ‖ ‖ ‖	99	‖ ‖ ‖ ‖ ‖	124	‖ ‖ ‖ ‖ ‖
25	‖ ‖ ‖ ‖ ‖	50	‖ ‖ ‖ ‖ ‖	75	‖ ‖ ‖ ‖ ‖	100	‖ ‖ ‖ ‖ ‖	125	‖ ‖ ‖ ‖ ‖